INCORPORATION AND BUSINESS GUIDE FOR WASHINGTON

INCORPORATION AND BUSINESS GUIDE FOR WASHINGTON

How to form your own corporation

Victoria Van Hof, Attorney

Self-Counsel Press Inc.
a subsidiary of
International Self-Counsel Press Ltd.
U.S.A. Canada

Printed in Canada

First edition: May, 1978
Second edition: October, 1981
Third edition: December, 1984
Fourth edition: October, 1987
Fifth edition: July, 1990
Sixth edition: December, 1993
Seventh edition: July, 1996

Cataloguing in Publication Data

Van Hof, Victoria.
Incorporation and business guide for Washington

(Self-counsel legal series)
First-2nd eds. by Harold B. Coe.
First-5th eds. have title: Incorporation & business guide for Washington.
ISBN 1-55180-066-7

1. Incorporation — Washington (State) — Popular works. I. Coe, Harold B., 1937- Incorporation & business guide for Washington. II. Title. III. Title: Incorporation & business guide for Washington. IV. Series.
KFW213.Z9C64 1996 346.797'06622 C95-911199-9

Self-Counsel Press Inc.
a subsidiary of
International Self-Counsel Press Ltd.

1704 N. State Street
Bellingham, Washington 98225

1481 Charlotte Road
North Vancouver, British Columbia V7J 1H1

CONTENTS

SAMPLES

TABLES

AVAILABLE FROM THE PUBLISHER

In order to incorporate your business, you will need to file certain forms. You may type these yourself, but it is easier and quicker to use pre-printed forms.

INCORPORATION FORMS — $12.95

The practice has grown in the legal profession of using certain standard printed forms which ease the typing load considerably. The pre-packaged forms are available where you bought this book or you may use the order form on page xii. The cost of the package is $12.95 plus tax and handling. The kit of forms includes:

- 2 Applications for Reservation of Name
- 3 sets of Articles of Incorporation (1 working copy; 2 for filing)
- 2 Consents to Action of Board of Directors
- 2 sets of Bylaws

ADDITIONAL ITEMS AVAILABLE FROM THE PUBLISHER

Seal with corporate name — $31.50

The seal should not be ordered until you have received your Certificate of Incorporation.

Minute book — $18.00

Company payee stamp — $6.00

(This is a one-line stamp with your company name. It is used to stamp the front of checks that you receive from your customers.)

Deposit stamp — $9.25

("For deposit only" and your company name — 2 lines. To be used for stamping the backs of checks.)

Company name and address stamp — 3 lines — $8.95 4 lines — $10.95

(To be used for general correspondence and miscellaneous functions.)

(Prices subject to change without notice.)

Send to:

Self-Counsel Press Inc.
1704 N. State Street
Bellingham, Washington 98225

(Clip and mail)

ORDER FORM

Please send the following items prepaid:

________ Incorporation forms kit		$12.95
________ Seal with corporate name		$31.50
Please include year of incorporation for company seal: 19______		
________ Minute book		$18.00
________ Payee stamp (1 line)		$ 6.00
________ Deposit stamp (2 lines)		$ 9.25
________ Corporate name and address stamp	(3 lines)	$ 8.95
	(4 lines)	$10.95
TOTAL		$________
Washington residents add sales tax		$________
Add $2.50 for postage and handling		$ 2.50

TOTAL to be forwarded by check or money order, or $________

billed to ❑ MasterCard ❑ Visa

MasterCard/Visa number ____________________ Expiry date:__________

Signature____

Please send the items checked above to:

Mr./Ms.: ____

Address: ____

City:______________ State:______________ Zip Code:__________

Telephone: ____

Name of corporation: ____

Corporation address (for stamp) if not same as above:______________

____

Please check your seals and stamps upon receipt. We will not be responsible for errors reported more than 30 days after mailing.

(Printed in Canada)

NOTICE TO READERS

Laws are constantly changing. Every effort is made to keep this publication as current as possible. However, the author, the publisher, and the vendor of this book make no representation or warranties regarding the outcome or the use to which the information in this book is put and are not assuming any liability for any claims, losses, or damages arising out of the use of this book. The reader should not rely on the author or the publisher of this book for any professional advice. Please be sure that you have the most recent edition.

Note: The fees quoted in this book are correct at the date of publication. However, fees are subject to change without notice. For current fees, please check with the Corporations Division or appropriate government office nearest you.

PREFACE

Why are you interested in incorporating? Probably because of your accountant's suggestion or because you have heard vague references from your friends and business associates about the advantages of having a company or maybe because you just think it's the thing to do.

Whatever your reason is, you are probably confused and perhaps even frustrated at the idea of having to spend hundreds of dollars for something you know nothing about and for which you have trouble seeing the benefits that are supposed to accrue to you.

If so, this book is for you. For a relatively small investment, this publication will clear away those uncertainties and explain in simple, layperson's language the whys and wherefores of incorporating and, in addition, will save you hundreds of dollars in lawyer's fees.

However, there are some areas where this book cannot replace your lawyer or accountant.

Specifically, if you are setting up a business where there are opposing interests, or if you are involved in intricate and complex debt or share issues, it is essential that proper counsel be retained. If you are not involved in such a situation, by following the procedures set out in this manual, you will save a substantial amount ($500 to $1,000) in legal fees for incorporating a company.

In any event, if the business is successful, whether you seek competent professional help prior to incorporation or not, you will undoubtedly require the services of a qualified accountant following incorporation. Doing the books yourself is both dangerous and, in the long run, expensive.

This publication is not meant to circumvent or to derogate from the value of professional help. It is meant as an aid to persons who desire a simple incorporation and find that the money spent for professional fees may be better spent elsewhere, or for those who simply want to become acquainted with the legal and practical implications of a limited company.

By following the recommendations and directions of this book and adapting its samples and forms and letters to your needs, you should be able to form your own Washington corporation with a minimum of expense and minimum of legal assistance. There is absolutely no legal prohibition against a layperson's preparing and filing Articles of Incorporation if it is done for his or her own benefit, nor against preparing certificates of stock, conducting directors' and shareholders' meetings, and preparing minutes of meetings.

1
WHY INCORPORATE? METHODS OF DOING BUSINESS

To answer the question "why form a corporation?" properly, it is necessary to have an understanding of and insight into the nature and implications of business forms.

If you are already carrying on business and are not incorporated, you must be operating either as a sole proprietor or as a partner in a business. There are only three ways to carry on any business: as a sole proprietorship, a partnership, or an incorporated company. These encompass every type of business, from the smallest corner grocery store to General Motors.

Some of the important features of each of these business structures will be examined to enable you to study and evaluate the advantages, disadvantages, and liabilities of each.

There are also special entities such as organizations engaged in charitable or semi-charitable enterprises, but these do not concern us here and will not be discussed.

a. THE SOLE PROPRIETORSHIP

The sole proprietorship form of business is the oldest, simplest, and least complicated type of business structure. It is simply an individual who engages in business for himself or herself.

1. Advantages of a sole proprietorship

The principal characteristic and advantage of the sole proprietorship is the absence of a formal "business organization," that is, the absence of the need to file formal papers of organization or enter into formal agreements with other parties. By not having to file formal papers of organization, a sole proprietorship also is able to avoid many government regulatory and reporting requirements (and related expenses) imposed upon corporations.

The sole proprietor may sell or otherwise dispose of the business in any manner he or she sees fit, at any time, without obtaining the consent, agreement, or permission of another person. Since the sole proprietor has the complete power of decision, he or she may simply close the doors, liquidate the business assets, and stop doing business. Also, the owner is not subject to any liabilities or debts created by others.

The sole proprietor avoids a "double tax" on earnings distributed to the owner-shareholders, and any losses which may be anticipated in the early years of business operations can be set off against other income. (The double tax situation arises in a corporation because a corporation must first pay tax on its net earnings and then its shareholders must pay tax on any dividends that are distributed. Working partners who earn salaries are required to pay tax on the money earned through the corporation.)

2. Disadvantages of a sole proprietorship

Probably the major disadvantage to this type of business organization is that the sole proprietor is personally responsible for the performance of all contracts, the fulfillment of all business obligations, and the payment of all debts and taxes incurred in the operation of the business. All of the sole owner's personal assets may be seized for the payment of business obligations and taxes.

Also the sole proprietor is personally responsible and liable for all of the acts of his or her employees in the performance of their duties in carrying out their work.

This relationship is called a "principal and agent" relationship. The sole owner is viewed as the principal, with employees as agents. The significance of this relationship can be seen in this example: if an employee operates an automobile, owned either by the employer or by the employee, and in the course of the employer's business he or she causes an accident through negligent driving, the employer, as well as the employee, is liable for damages. For protection, the sole owner should carry adequate public liability insurance including non-owned automobile insurance. Workers' compensation insurance must also be carried, or penalties could result.

Employees acting within the scope of their authorized duties can make their employer responsible for carrying out the terms of an oral or written contract whether or not their employer consents or approves of the terms.

In addition, the sole owner is also personally responsible for the payment of all social security taxes, withholding taxes, federal and state unemployment insurance, industrial insurance premiums, and medical and pension plan premiums that are deducted from an employee's wages, as well as for making his or her own contribution to these various plans.

A further disadvantage of the sole proprietorship is that its usefulness is limited by the fact that capital investment, which is essential to the effective initiation of any business, is confined to the owner's personal resources.

Any profits of the business are taxed as an ordinary income to the owner and he or she is not entitled to the fringe benefits afforded corporate employees under our tax laws.

Finally the business is subject to disintegration upon the death or incapacity of the owner. Thus estate planning can become complex.

3. Doing business under a name other than your own

As sole proprietor, you are not required to conduct business under your own name. An assumed or trade business name may be used so long as it is not in conflict with any existing trade business name. You may wish to use a name descriptive of your business or locale, or you may simply want to avoid the use of your own name.

The practical significance of all this is that if you want to sue someone, you cannot sue in the name of your business, because it is not a legally formed entity. If you wanted to sue someone you would have to phrase the claim as follows:

"Sam Slick doing business as
Slipshod Industries."

In order to avoid raising a presumption of fraud in your business dealings, or in obtaining credit, file a trade name statement in the Office of the County Clerk of the county where you conduct business. Any changes in the name should be followed by the filing of a new statement.

A certificate showing the registration of your business name must always be produced before you can initiate a lawsuit on behalf of your business.

b. THE GENERAL PARTNERSHIP

A partnership is defined as an association of two or more persons to carry on as co-owners of a business for profit. Like a proprietorship, a partnership is not a separate legal entity apart from its partners or members. It is an association of two or more persons who have agreed to engage in a business venture.

A general partnership is created by an agreement that can be oral, written, or implied by conduct among individuals who associate themselves as partners for the purpose of engaging in a business enterprise.

A general partnership agreement is not required by law to be in writing; it may simply be an oral understanding (that is sometimes evidenced by a handshake) followed by performance of the terms of the understanding. However it is strongly recommended that the agreement of the partners be put into writing and signed by all partners. When a partnership agreement is put into writing there can be less misunderstanding of —

(a) the business purposes of the general partnership,

(b) the organization of the business,

(c) the duties and authority of each partner,

(d) the amount of capital each partner has invested in the business (this is called the participating percentage),

(e) the sharing of profits,

(f) the termination of the general partnership, and

(g) the transition of interest from departing partners to remaining partners.

It is important to realize that you may be considered to be in partnership with someone even though you have made no formal declaration of such a partnership. This is because a partnership can be created by the relationship of the parties, and not by any formal agreement or act.

Unless a formal partnership document exists, there is no single established test as to what constitutes a partnership, although the following criteria are applied to a relationship to serve as guidelines in determining whether or not it is a partnership.

(a) Is there a sharing of profits and losses?

(b) Do any of the parties act as agents for others?

(c) Is there any property held in joint tenancy?

(d) Is there any implication of partnership on your firm's letterhead or in its correspondence?

(e) Is the nature of the working relationship that of a partnership?

(f) Do the parties deal with the public or "hold themselves out" as partners?

1. Advantages of a partnership

The most important advantage of partnerships is that knowledge, ability, and experience are shared among several persons. The partnership as a whole gains from drawing upon the strengths and financial resources of each partner.

The partnership also generally enjoys the advantages of a proprietorship that were discussed earlier.

2. Disadvantages of a partnership

The chief danger of doing business as a general partnership is the risk of *unlimited partnership liability* that each individual partner assumes on becoming a partner.

The property of the general partnership is available for the payment of all the debts and obligations incurred by the general partnership, and all payable taxes. If the general partnership property is insufficient to pay the debts, obligations, and taxes of the general partnership, then each of the partners becomes *personally* responsible for paying *all* the debts, obligations, and taxes of the general partnership. This means that a partner, as an individual, becomes liable for the entire amount owed by the general partnership and not just a proportionate share of the debts, obligations, and taxes. However, it is only after the general partnership assets have been exhausted that the individual partners may be compelled to pay the partnership debts, obligations, and taxes personally. In this case, each partner's personal assets become vulnerable to satisfy a judgment obtained against the general partnership and partners. In addition, each individual partner is personally responsible for the business actions of all partners acting on behalf of the general partnership.

3. Rights and obligations of partners

The Washington law governing partnerships is found in Title 25 of the Revised Code of Washington (RCW). While it provides that all partners have equal rights in the management and conduct of the general business, a general partnership agreement should specify details of authority and duties. Without a clear statement of the authority and duties assigned to each of the individual partners, misunderstandings and confusion could easily result.

No partner is entitled to receive a salary or wages for acting on behalf of the general partnership unless the general partnership agreement specifies such payments, or the partner is engaged as an employee. Each partner has the right to inspect and examine the books of the general partnership at any reasonable time, regardless of personal authority or duties. Each partner is entitled to the repayment, at the time agreed upon, of loans made to the general partnership or advances made on behalf of the general partnership.

4. What terms should be in a partnership agreement?

A general partnership agreement should cover at least the following subjects:

(a) Name of general partnership

(b) Names and addresses of all general partners

(c) Statement of business to be conducted and the place where it is to be carried on

(d) Time of commencement and duration of the general partnership

(e) Statement of initial capital investment to be made by each partner in the general partnership, and the additional amount to be assessed to each partner if additional capital is required

(f) Statement as to the duties and services to be performed by each partner, and the compensation to be paid if a partner is employed by the general partnership

(g) Provision for drawing accounts of partners to be deducted from their share of profits

(h) Statement about how profits and losses are to be divided among the partners

(i) Provision for such functions as keeping books and accounts and taking inventory (It is recommended that an accountant be retained to set up a bookkeeping system.)

(j) Name of bank in which general partnership funds will be deposited, and the names of partners authorized to sign checks

(k) Consideration of the effect of withdrawal, death, incapacity, or insanity of a partner in relationship to dissolution of the general partnership

(l) Buy-sell agreements

(m) Arbitration agreement in the event of a serious disagreement between the partners

(n) Dissolution of the general partnership

Note: See also the section on "Doing business under a name other than your own," as the same rules apply to partnerships.

This list is not meant to be all-inclusive. Other subjects may need to be included for your individual situation.

5. How is a partnership dissolved?

The law concerning partnerships provides that a partnership dissolves automatically on the death, retirement, or incapacity of a partner, unless other provisions are made in the general partnership agreement.

The general partnership agreement may provide for continuance of the general partnership regardless of any of the above causes of dissolution except bankruptcy or a court decree dissolving the partnership.

Upon the election of the partners to dissolve the general partnership, the general partnership will continue to exist after such action has been taken until all the affairs of the general partnership have been wound up and settled, and its debts paid. The agreement or election to dissolve the partnership does not relieve the partners from the possibility of individual personal liability for the payment of the general partnership's debts and taxes.

Winding up the affairs of the general partnership means that its obligations must be settled, its debts and taxes paid, and its remaining assets distributed to the partners or personal representatives of a deceased partner.

To ensure that all creditors of the general partnership have knowledge of the dissolution, each creditor should be notified by mail that the general partnership has been dissolved and that no person has authority to act or to incur obligations for the general partnership.

c. THE LIMITED PARTNERSHIP

A limited partnership is a partnership of one or more general partners and one or more limited partners. A limited partner is not personally liable for the debts of the partnership. Limited partners can lose only their investment in a business.

Like general partnerships, limited partnerships are governed by statute if there is no formal written agreement.

As a general statement, partners in a limited partnership share equally in profits and losses. However, neither a partner's share in the profits and losses nor the partnership interests of the partners need be equal. The limited partnership agreement should specify each partner's proportionate share of profits and losses.

The assets of the partnership belong to the limited partnership as a whole. During the life of the partnership, the individual partners do not, as such, have the right of ownership to specific assets of the partnership, but each owns only his or her proportionate interest in the property of the limited partnership.

When the partnership is dissolved, each partner is entitled to receive his or her share of the partnership property.

1. Advantages of a limited partnership

The purpose and special advantage of a limited partnership under RCW Chapter 25.10 is that it constitutes a form of business enterprise other than a corporation in which persons can invest their money without becoming liable as general partners for all debts of the partnership, thus giving a limited partner a position of limited liability comparable to that of a corporate shareholder.

A limited partner is not liable as a general partner in most instances, unless, in addition to the exercise of rights and powers as a limited partner, he or she takes part in the control of the business.

2. Disadvantages of a limited partnership

A limited partner, at the risk of being held liable as a general partner, may not in any way participate in the management or control of the partnership business.

Also, there are specific regulations concerning the firm name under which the business may be conducted. A limited partner's surname cannot be used as part of the business name because he or she will be liable as a general partner to creditors who extend credit to the partnership without actually knowing that the limited partner is not a general partner.

Under the limited partnership provisions of Chapter 25.10, a corporation may act as a general partner. Because of the similarity of a limited partnership investment in corporate stock, there is always the danger that a limited partnership will be treated as an "association" that is taxable as a corporation. If you are contemplating a limited partnership arrangement with a corporate general partner, you really should consider applying for an advance ruling from the Internal Revenue Service (IRS) on whether or not your limited partnership is a partnership or a corporation for federal tax purposes.

3. How to form a limited partnership

Unlike a general partnership, which is not required by law to have an agreement in writing, or comply with any particular formalities, the limited partnership must strictly comply with the requirements of the law (Chapter 25.10). All partners must sign and acknowledge the Certificate of Limited Partnership.

Two signed copies of the Certificate of Limited Partnership and of any certificates of amendment or cancellation (or of any judicial decree of amendment or cancellation) must be delivered to the Secretary of State.

Because the formation, preparation, and conduct of a limited partnership is complicated and technical, it is recommended that an attorney be retained to prepare the Certificate of Limited Partnership and to advise the general and limited partners of their rights, duties, obligations, and limitations.

4. How to dissolve a limited partnership

A limited partnership is like a general partnership in that the death, retirement, or incapacity of a general partner will automatically dissolve a limited partnership unless other provisions are made in the certificate.

The Certificate of Limited Partnership may also provide the time for which the limited partnership shall exist, and the date when the limited partnership will automatically dissolve.

Whenever a limited partnership is dissolved, its affairs must be settled; its debts, obligations, and taxes paid; and the remaining cash and other assets distributed. Distribution is made first to limited partners in accordance with their proportionate shares, and the balance of the cash and other assets is then distributed to the general partners. When a limited partnership dissolves, the Certificate of Limited Partnership must be canceled.

You should retain an attorney for advice in the procedures necessary to terminate the existence of the limited partnership.

d. THE LIMITED LIABILITY COMPANY

The limited liability company is a relatively new form of business organization established by Washington law in 1994 in Chapter 25.15. The purpose of this form of business organization is to provide the limited liability benefits of a corporation while providing the tax advantages of a partnership. The limited liability company is particularly suited for professional practices and businesses. For more information, see *How to Form and Operate a Limited Liability Company*, another title in the Self-Counsel Series.

e. THE CORPORATION

A corporation is a distinct legal entity; an artificial person quite different from the people who are its shareholders. When you incorporate, you actually create a new person in the eyes of the law. The assets and debts of a corporation belong to it — not to the individual shareholders.

Because of this characteristic, there are no major advantages to the individuals who incorporate their business.

A stock corporation is one organized to carry on a business for profit, to distribute profits as dividends to its shareholders, and to distribute its assets to them when it is dissolved.

Another type of corporation commonly formed in Washington is the non stock or nonprofit corporation, which does not distribute its gains or profits to its members. It is a corporation in which individuals associate themselves together for religious, charitable, social, or educational purposes, or for rendering services subject to laws and regulations applicable to the particular class of nonprofit corporation or line of activity.

The majority of Washington stock corporations are "close stock corporations" which means that the stock is owned by one person or a small number of people, and these same people are also directors. This type of corporation is the principal subject of this book.

1. Advantages of a corporation

(a) Greater source of capital

There is potentially a greater source of capital available than in a partnership. Since the company is a "person" separate from its shareholders, people may invest money in it without accepting any further responsibility for conducting the company business and without worrying about becoming liable for the debts of the company.

Ownership in a public corporation is freely transferable by the sale and transfer of stock certificates. Shares in a "close" corporation are also transferable but may have certain restrictions attached to their transfer.

(b) Perpetual existence

Unlike a sole proprietorship or a partnership, the existence of the corporation is perpetual and will not cease upon the death or incapacity of any shareholder.

Since the company is a separate "person," it does not expire when the shareholders die. Substantial estate planning benefits result from this aspect of companies.

(c) Limited liability

The major nontax advantage of the corporate form is the limited liability of the shareholders for the debts of the business. Generally, a shareholder's risk of loss is limited to the amount invested in the corporation, and the debts of the corporation cannot be satisfied out of the personal assets of the shareholder.

This means that your liability as a shareholder is limited to the amount of money you owe the company (i.e., for shares), and does not include the amounts of money which your company itself owes to its creditors.

This is obviously an important advantage to you. There are, however, certain limitations, the most important one being that, in many instances, creditors, particularly banks, will not extend credit to a small company without your personal guarantee as its shareholder. However, if you do not personally guarantee your company's loans then your liability as a shareholder is limited to what you have invested in the company and the amount you owe for unpaid shares, if any.

The following examples illustrate the foregoing principles:

Example 1

John Doe and Jack Doe carry on business as a partnership known as J & J Industries.

J & J Industries incurs debts of $25,000 and has assets of $10,000.

A creditor successfully petitions J & J Industries into bankruptcy or simply gets a judgment against J & J Industries.

All the assets of John Doe and Jack Doe, as individuals, including possibly their homes, cars, etc., may be executed against to repay the $15,000 debt incurred by the partnership over and above its assets.

Example 2

John Doe and Jack Doe carry on business as a corporation known as J & J Industries Incorporated, with John Doe and Jack Doe the only shareholders, each having purchased 250 shares at $1 each.

J & J Industries Incorporated incurs debts of $25,000. The assets of the company are considered to have a market value of $10,000. Thus, the assets and equity of J & J Industries Incorporated equal $10,500.

A creditor successfully petitions J & J Industries Incorporated into bankruptcy.

The creditors can realize $10,500 on the assets and equity of the company but they have no rights against John and Jack as individuals, regardless of the value of personal assets that John and Jack may own outside the company. The creditors are creditors of the company, not of John and Jack.

In addition, banks often require the owner of a business to take out life insurance for himself or herself as a condition to obtaining a loan. The type of insurance involved is almost always term insurance, but the important point to remember is that the premium on this type of transaction is a *company* expense. If you have paid for this personally, you are entitled to be reimbursed by the company.

(d) Community recognition

An incorporated company usually has more credibility in the eyes of the banks, creditors, and customers. You are taken seriously if you have gone to the trouble and expense of incorporating, which indicates that you have long-range plans for your business.

(e) Tax advantages

The tax advantages of incorporating are so important that a whole chapter has been devoted to the subject (see chapter 3).

2. Disadvantages of a corporation

In order not to appear overly biased, I think it only fair to mention some disadvantages of incorporating.

Operating through a company does entail extra paperwork. You have to file incorporation documents and minutes. You have to file two tax returns: one for your company and one for yourself.

Since the corporation is a creature of law, it is subject to state regulatory and reporting requirements and tax laws. As such, it must qualify to do business in each foreign jurisdiction (i.e., state).

There may be additional government paperwork to do from time to time, which could be avoided by operating as a sole proprietor. (They always seem to find a company quicker.)

Some of the disadvantages of a corporation relate to the ease of transfer of ownership. Because ownership can be transferred so easily, incompatible investors may become co-owners of the business. This is particularly true in a small, closely held corporation. But such a problem may be solved through the use of a buy-sell agreement, illustrated in chapter 5.

Finally, for corporations, there are extra organizational costs and fees required by law, payable to the Secretary of State. Also, yearly fees have to be paid to keep the corporation in good standing.

f. SUMMARY

The book began with the question, "why form a corporation?" The foregoing comparison of the rights, liabilities, and duties attached to the sole proprietorship, general partnership, limited partnership, and corporation business structures should answer that question.

To summarize, there are three main legal forms an organization can take. These forms and their individual characteristics are outlined briefly below for quick reference.

Proprietorship

(a) Unincorporated

(b) Owned by one person

(c) Creditors have a legal claim on both the investment in the business and the personal assets of the owner

Partnership

(a) Unincorporated

(b) Each general partner has unlimited liability. In a limited partnership, a limited partner's liability is restricted to his or her investment in the business

(c) The acts of one partner in the course of the management of the business are binding upon the other partners

(d) The partnership dissolves upon the death or withdrawal of any partner, or upon the acceptance of a new partner

(e) Creditors have a legal claim on both the investments in the business and the personal assets of the general partners

Corporation

(a) Incorporated by Article of Incorporation filed with the Secretary of State

(b) Exists as a separate legal entity

(c) Shareholders are liable only to the extent of their investment in the business

(d) Usually possesses tax advantages

2
PRE-INCORPORATION CHECKLIST

a. INTRODUCTION

Before starting and investing in a business about which you know very little, it is imperative that you learn as much as you can about that business beforehand. Otherwise, it can prove to be an expensive and disturbing undertaking. If you are planning to go into a new business, my personal recommendation is that you first gain experience.

Careful planning in advance of entering any business is most essential. Gain as much knowledge as you can. Surprise can hurt you badly. In this regard you might well refer to *Starting a Successful Business on the West Coast*, another title in the Self-Counsel series. It is available at your local bookstore and explains all you need to know about state and federal licensing regulations, how to finance a business, where to locate it, and so on.

By following the recommendations and directions of this book and adapting its samples of forms and letters to your needs, you should be able to form your own Washington corporation with a minimum of expense and legal assistance.

There is absolutely no legal prohibition against a layperson who prepares and files Articles of Incorporation if it is done for his or her own benefit. Nor is there any legal prohibition against preparing certificates of stock, conducting directors' and shareholders' meetings, or preparing minutes of meetings.

b. WHERE TO INCORPORATE

Since a corporation is an artificial person in the eyes of the law, it must be "born" or incorporated in the state where it starts into business. Following expansion it can be registered in other states and thereby qualify to do business as a "foreign" corporation in that state. Once you expand outside your home state, you must follow the registration procedures for every state in which you intend to do business.

Note: What constitutes "doing business" in a foreign state is often a complex issue. For example, setting up an office in Portland would certainly mean your corporation would need to be registered in Oregon. However, what if you merely order goods from out of state on a regular basis? This probably would not constitute "doing business" in that particular state *unless* your corporation took delivery in that state or you had to sue the supplier in the courts of that state.

In summary, remember that to become legally recognized in any state other than the one in which you incorporated, you are required to register your corporation. Registration requirements are something to watch out for and be aware of *at all times*.

c. WHO MAY INCORPORATE

The law is that any person or group of persons over the age of 18 may act as incorporators by paying the proper fees and completing and filing the required articles — which includes details of the registered office and registered agent — with the Secretary of State's office.

Washington law allows the formation of one-person corporations. The same person may hold all the following positions: sole director, sole shareholder, and sole officer (i.e., president and secretary).

The one-person corporation allowance recognizes the fact that many people are in business solely with and for themselves. Rather than requiring that there be a "nominal" second shareholder who performs no real function and serves no purpose, it was considered desirable to allow a single person to have the advantages of incorporation.

The procedures for incorporating a one-person corporation are the same as those for incorporating any close corporation, and the required annual meetings can be held with only one person in attendance.

d. CLASSES OF SHARES

A share represents a proportionate interest in the net value of the corporation (i.e., what would remain if all the company's liabilities to outside creditors were fully paid).

A shareholder, in addition to his or her interest in the corporation's net value, has a number of contractual rights as set out in the corporate articles and bylaws, as well as those rights set out in the Washington Business Corporation Act.

Generally speaking, shares can have innumerable rights and restrictions attached to them. Therefore, a class of shares can be any set of shares which have certain rights attached to them, which are different from those attached to another set of shares.

In the vast majority of new close corporations, it is not necessary at the outset to place special rights and restrictions on your issued shares. When you start your corporation, you should incorporate with and issue "common shares" to all of the incorporators, so that all the shareholders of the company have equal rights to vote and to receive dividends.

Unless you receive sound professional advice and know what you are doing, it is wise to avoid different classes of shares at the beginning. Only those small business corporations with common shares can take advantage of the sometimes favorable tax treatment offered by subchapter S and section 1244 of the Internal Revenue Code (see chapter 3), although there may be differences in voting rights among the shares of common stock.

Later, when your company becomes successful and you feel there is a need for a more complicated share structure, you will be in a position to seek competent legal advice to carry out the alterations correctly and to design your capital structure to minimize tax and control advantages. Then you might wish to create a different class of shares which, when issued to shareholders, will give them the right to receive dividends before holders of any other class of shares, or which have cumulative dividend rights, or rights to be redeemed by the corporation. You might refer to the new class of shares as "preferred" shares to distinguish them from the other shares that you first issued.

Remember, it is much easier to add rights and restrictions later than it is to attach them in the beginning and later have to buy them up or strip them.

e. KINDS OF SHARES

This is an area which causes some problems for a do-it-yourselfer, but it is easy to understand once you realize that there are only two kinds of shares: par value and no par value. Both kinds of shares may be issued in different classes, e.g., you can have preferred no par value shares and cumulative par value shares.

There is really no practical difference between the two kinds of shares. Someone

— usually a lawyer who seeks to "make it easier for a layperson to understand" — just assigns an arbitrary value to the shares in relation to the worth of the company.

The key thing to remember about par value shares is that the issue price is fixed by the Board of Directors and the shares cannot be issued for less than the set amount (issuing shares at more than the par value is all right, however). For example, a share with a par value of $1 cannot be issued for less than $1. On the other hand, shares with no par value may be issued for any amount. (A share is first *issued*, then it can be *transferred* for any price between shareholders.)

The distinction between par and no par value shares has little real significance because immediately after any type of share is issued, its value will rise or fall depending on its true market value. And on any resale, par value shares can be sold for any price — even if it is less than the original issuing price.

In other words, the worth of a corporation's enterprise depends not on what type of shares it issues, but on what its net worth is in hard cash value. Many lawyers issue par value shares because they are more easily understood by the layperson. However, shares without par value are a better barometer because they reflect more accurately the true worth of a business, whereas par value shares attempt to impose an artificial value, which has no meaning after the initial issue.

The equation "Net worth = Value of shares" is always true. For example, if you wish to invest $1 in a corporation via the purchase of shares, it does not make any difference whether you receive one share with a par value of $1 or 100 no par value shares at 1¢ each. The value of the share or shares will rise or fall in relation to the net worth of the corporation. In most cases, you should incorporate with no par value shares so that you are not restricted to issuing your shares to incorporators or original shareholders for a set price, as you would have to do with par value shares.

The price at which you issue no par value shares to yourselves as incorporators depends strictly on the amount of equity capital you wish to establish.

In Washington, a corporation must have $500 in equity capital prior to engaging in business. As long as this minimum is met, it is not advisable to invest a large sum in the equity capital of a corporation.

f. HOW MANY SHARES SHOULD YOU ISSUE?

Every business needs capital to begin operations. Capital flows into a business in two ways:

(a) By investing in shares, i.e., equity capital

(b) By lending money to the business in some form or other, e.g., shareholder loans, bonds, debentures

There are definite advantages to establishing the capital of a business through loans, as opposed to buying shares, especially in a high-risk business such as a newly incorporated partnership or proprietorship.

The first is that capital "loaned" to the corporation, as opposed to "invested" in the corporation, can be repaid at any time tax-free, i.e., a loan to the corporation repaid to a shareholder is not income to the shareholder. On the other hand, money invested in shares cannot be repaid while the corporation is operating. Therefore, any withdrawal of capital by the owners must be done through payment of dividends which are taxable to the corporation and its shareholders, unless a subchapter S election is made. (In that event, the corporation is taxed as if it were a proprietorship. See chapter 3 for further discussion.)

Secondly, if the new corporation is near financial collapse, a shareholder loan ranks equally with the other creditors when dividing up the remainder of the assets and ahead of repayment to the shareholders for money invested in shares. Common shareholders rarely see any proceeds when a corporation goes bankrupt.

However, care must be taken in determining a proper ratio. If too much is "loaned," the IRS may declare the capital to be an investment, thereby making any repayment a dividend.

Another reason for not issuing all the shares is that they have to be paid for at the time they are issued. And anyway, there is no good reason to put a large amount of capital into the corporation by way of share purchase. Washington law requires that a minimum of $500 be advanced as equity through the purchase of shares before the corporation can commence business. Therefore, this sum should be regarded as the basic minimum and there is usually little advantage in financing the corporation by larger amounts of share capital.

In addition, if all of the shares are issued immediately after incorporation and if a new shareholder wishes to join existing shareholders without obtaining their shares, an amendment to the articles must be filed to increase the amount of authorized capital. The procedure for amending your articles is explained in chapter 11 and is not very difficult. Nevertheless, a little thought before you divide up the total amount of authorized capital can save time and effort later.

A final and most important reason is that if your business is successful, you may wish to bring in other "partners" who want to invest in the business. At that time a valuation of the amount of "equity" you have in the business will have to be made. This should be done by your accountant.

Equity is defined as assets minus liabilities and represents the net worth of the business. In Samples #1 and #2 it can be seen that it makes no difference how many total shares are issued as long as your position with regard to other shareholders is not altered. Also, by keeping most of the shares in the treasury, you will be flexible enough to meet new corporate developments.

In the following samples, you will see that I have purposely simplified matters by deducting shareholders' contributions because this is like transferring money from one hand to the next in a small, nonpublic corporation. I have also deliberately ignored the "good will" or capitalization of earnings factor which merely serves to place a multiple factor on the net earnings.

You will see that, in each of these examples, John and Jack Doe's business is worth the same on a net return basis, no matter how many shares were issued.

Another major problem with issuing shares arises when two equal partners wish to bring in a third partner on an equal basis. If John and Jack Doe each have 50 shares, we could have John and Jack each transfer 16⅔ shares to their new partner, cousin Heather. The problem with transferring an equal percentage of each shareholder's holdings to the newcomer is that John and Jack would be forced to deal with the annoying problem of fractional shares as each would have 33⅓ shares.

Furthermore, if the shares were transferred to Heather at a profit, John and Jack would be liable for capital gains tax. In order to avoid the fractional share problem, Jack and John could take 25 shares each from the treasury and then transfer them to Heather so all partners would have 50 shares.

Again, if Heather has to pay Jack and John more than the shares were issued for, Jack and John would be liable for capital gains tax on the profit realized. No capital gains tax would be payable if Heather paid the same price for her shares as Jack and John paid into the company treasury when the shares were issued, although the tax department may regard this as a taxable benefit received by Heather and tax her accordingly.

The same result could be achieved by simply issuing 50 shares to Heather directly from the treasury at the fair market price agreed upon. No capital gains tax whatever is payable because the money simply flows into the capital account of the company. However, John and Jack might not be too happy, as they receive no direct benefit for bringing Heather in. They do have her contribution to the work effort, though, as well as her money to finance the company's activities.

I hope that this example makes it clear that it is simpler to avoid complicated partial share arrangements by issuing additional shares directly to the new shareholder, or by issuing extra shares to existing members for transfer to the newcomer.

I have already covered the advantages of financing the corporation by using loans rather than equity capital. To lend the corporation capital, simply write the company a check and make a note on the check and bank deposit slip that it is a shareholder loan. Your accountant or bookkeeper will make the proper entries from your check stub.

In summary, there is no particular advantage to issuing all the shares unless you are involved in a complicated share control problem. As this is the only advantage, and there are several disadvantages to capitalizing through personal investment in share capital, it is wise to issue a minimum number of shares to begin with, say 50 to 100 depending upon the number of persons involved.

SAMPLE #1
BALANCE SHEET
(Where 50,000 shares issued)

J & J PERSONNEL INCORPORATED

ASSETS		**LIABILITIES**	
Cash	$50,500	Note to the bank	$2,000
Inventory	4,000	Shareholder loan	3,000
Building	5,000		
Total assets	$59,500	**Total liabilities**	$5,000
		Net worth	
		Capital stock authorized — 50,000 shares	
		Issued 50,000 shares at $1 each 25,000 to A for $25,000 and 25,000 to B for $25,000	$50,000
		Earned surplus	$ 4,500
		Total equity	$54,500
		Total liabilities and equity	$59,500

Note: If the business is wound up, both A's and B's shares are worth $54,500, but as $50,000 is their own money, the net gain is $2,250 (½ x 4,500), the same as in Sample #2.

SAMPLE #2
BALANCE SHEET
(Where 100 shares issued)

J & J PERSONNEL INCORPORATED

ASSETS		**LIABILITIES**	
Cash	$ 1,000	Note to the bank	$ 2,000
Inventory	4,000	Shareholder loan	3,000
Building	5,000		
Total assets	$10,000	**Total liabilities**	$ 5,000
		Net worth	
		Capital stock authorized — 50,000 shares	
		Issued 100 shares at $5 each 50 to A for $250 50 to B for $250	500
		Retained earnings	4,500
		Total equity	5,000
		Total liabilities and equity	$10,000

Note: A and B each have shares worth (in hard cash) $250, or a total of $500. But since $500 of the $5,000 equity is their own money, the net gain for each is $2,250 (½ x 4,500). Note also that shareholders' contributions are not included as this is like transferring money from one hand to the other. Similarly, "good will" has been ignored in both examples.

3

TAX ADVANTAGES OF INCORPORATION

a. GENERAL TAX BENEFITS

If the annual corporate income is less than $75,000, it will be taxed at a lower marginal rate than the same income would be taxed to an individual. Corporate tax rates are higher than individual tax rates, however, if the income exceeds $75,000. Corporations are taxed at 15% of income up to $50,000; 25% on the next $25,000; and 34% on income over $75,000.

Since the personal income tax rate declines rapidly at the lower end of the scale as well, significant tax savings can be made by splitting your income.

For example, if your business made $50,000 last year as a proprietorship, the entire amount would be brought into your personal income. The first $32,450 would be taxed at the 15% rate but the remainder would be taxed at the 28% rate (if you are married and filing a joint return). On the other hand, if you have incorporated, $17,550 (the amount over $32,450) could be left in the corporation for future use provided you can show a corporation benefit.

As long as salaries are reasonable, you can work any combination that keeps your total tax bill to a minimum. With the changing tax laws, you have much more flexibility. Additionally, corporations may exclude 70% (and, in some circumstances, 80% or 100%) of dividends received on qualified corporate owned stock.

Also, numerous and important benefits are available to you and your employees through incorporation. One of the most important employee "fringe benefits" is a health and accident plan. Under qualified plans, corporations can provide employees with medical, disability, and life insurance; child care benefits; educational assistance; group legal services; cafeteria plans; employer provided meals, lodging and transportation; and employee safety, longevity, and productivity rewards. All of these are deductible by the corporation and almost all can be excluded from the employee's personal income.

Another employee benefit is a deferred compensation plan. Retirement (deferred) compensation represents one of the best forms of tax shelter for a person who owns a controlling interest in a profitable, closely held corporation. Unlike oil drilling programs and other risky enterprises, the advantages of employee benefit plans include not only the immediate tax benefit but also possible conservation and growth of capital in a tax sheltered investment program.

Qualified plans provide the corporate employer and its employees with the following substantial tax advantages:

(a) Contributions to deferred compensation plans within certain limits are tax deductible by the employer.

(b) Benefits received by an employee are taxed only upon their receipt (usually at retirement when the employee is in a lower tax bracket) and are often subject to favorable tax treatment at that time.

(c) If a trust is established to fund the plan, its earnings are exempt from income tax. The income is taxed when the participant employee receives it, and often favorable tax rates or special averaging provisions apply.

(d) Death benefits, payable to anyone other than the deceased employee's estate, which arise from an employer's contributions to a qualified plan, are not included in the employee's gross estate for federal estate tax purposes.

(e) The corporate employer is able to reduce its earnings and profit by its contribution to a qualified plan of deferred compensation, and this helps to avoid accumulated earnings tax problems and reduce exposure to dividend tax treatment.

(f) By contributing funds to a separate employee benefit plan trust, the corporate employer may be able to decrease the net worth of the business and thereby reduce the value of its stock for gift and estate tax purposes.

(g) Corporations may also establish medical reimbursement plans for employees, their spouses, and their children, thereby having the corporation pay their medical expenses with tax deductible dollars.

From a planning standpoint, qualified plans should be an important consideration, particularly in the case of small, closely held family corporations. These advantages become most important when the business is prospering and the controlling shareholders are thinking about estate planning.

b. SUBCHAPTER S CORPORATIONS

The primary aim of subchapter S is to encourage the incorporation of small businesses and to allow certain advantages to small business corporations in an effort to ensure their success in the initial stages of operation.

When a corporation earns profits, it must pay a federal income tax on those profits. If the profits are distributed as dividends to shareholders, the shareholders must report the dividends as ordinary income and pay an income tax on the dividends. This results in double taxation of the same funds. This double taxation can be avoided if you take a salary equal to the amount of the profit, which in effect reduces the corporation profit to zero. (Thus there is no corporate tax.) This can be a tax advantage if the earnings are substantial. However, for most new businesses the bottom figure is very meager, at least for the first few years.

For this reason, Congress enacted subchapter S (sections 1361 to 1379 of the Internal Revenue Code). Subchapter S provides a means to avoid the double taxation. An S corporation is not generally required to pay any federal income tax on its profits (see discussion in section **3.**). The S corporation pays the profits, or dividends, directly to the individual shareholders who would then report the income as ordinary income and pay an income tax, thus eliminating the double income tax on the same funds. Losses are similarly passed on to the shareholders.

The S corporation income is, in effect, taxed at the individual rates rather than the corporate rate. Remember, this is an advantage only when corporate income is small. After the operation becomes a success and begins to generate larger taxable income, the shareholders may want to terminate the election in order to take advantage of the lower corporate tax rate.

1. Eligibility

To make an election under subchapter S, a corporation must be a domestic "small business corporation" that does not —

(a) have more than 35 shareholders (husband and wife are treated as one shareholder as long as they are married)

(b) have as a shareholder a person who is not an individual, other than an estate and certain trusts

(c) have a nonresident alien as a shareholder

(d) have more than one class of stock (differences in voting rights among shares of common stock are allowed)

Additionally, certain corporations are ineligible. These are:

(a) Financial institutions that are allowed a deduction for bad debts under IRC sections 585 and 593

(b) Insurance companies subject to taxation under subchapter L of the code

(c) A member of an affiliated group under IRC section 1504 (an electing corporation may not own 80% or more of each class of nonvoting stock of another active corporation)

(d) Corporations claiming a tax credit under IRC section 936 (concerning trade or business within a possession of the U.S.)

(e) A domestic international sales corporation as defined in IRC section 992

2. How to make a subchapter S election

If you wish to elect subchapter S status for your new corporation, the election must be made during the first two and one-half months of the corporation's taxable year. The taxable year of a small business corporation wishing to elect subchapter S status must be a "permitted taxable year." A permitted taxable year is either a year ending December 31 or an accounting period for which a business purpose is established to the satisfaction of the IRS.

A small business corporation must file a subchapter S election form with the Service Center where the corporation files its federal income tax return. The form, IRS 2553 (see Sample #3), must be filed together with the attached consents of all the shareholders.

Any future problems of proof will be avoided if you keep a copy of the form with a stamp from the IRS showing the date and time they received the election.

In addition, the Board of Directors should draw up minutes of a meeting, or consent resolutions in lieu of a meeting, in which subchapter S election is discussed and adopted. For example, the minutes shown in Sample #4 would be inserted into the Minutes of the Organizational Meeting of Directors of a new corporation if the directors decided to make the subchapter S election.

3. Subchapter S tax rules

An S corporation is treated in much the same manner as a partnership. The rules for computing an S corporation's income are essentially the same as those used to compute a partnership's income. Once computed, the income is passed through to the shareholders and taxed directly to them as if earned by them.

Although an S corporation is, therefore, not subject to the taxes normally imposed on corporations, special taxes are imposed in certain situations. If an S corporation earns too much passive income or has excessive capital gains, special taxes will be imposed. In addition, an S corporation must pay the tax that results from the recapture of any investment tax credits claimed while it was not an S corporation.

4. Termination or revocation of S corporation election

Once an election is made under subchapter S, it is effective for the taxable year of the corporation and for all succeeding years,

SAMPLE #3
SUBCHAPTER S ELECTION

Form **2553** (Rev. May 1983) Department of the Treasury Internal Revenue Service

Election by a Small Business Corporation
(Under section 1362 of the Internal Revenue Code)
▶ For Paperwork Reduction Act Notice, see page 1 of instructions.
▶ See separate instructions.

OMB No. 1545-0146

Note: *This election to be treated as an "S corporation" can be approved only if all the tests in Instruction B are met.*

Part I

Name of corporation (see instructions)	Employer identification number (see instructions)	Principal business activity and principal product or service (see instructions)
J & J PERSONNEL INC.	applied for	120S

Number and street	Election is to be effective for tax year beginning (month, day, year)
123 Business Avenue,	January 1, 19 9-

City or town, State and ZIP code	Number of shares issued and outstanding (see instructions)
Somewhere, WA 90000	500

Is the corporation the outgrowth or continuation of any form of predecessor? . . . . . ☐ Yes ☒ No

If "Yes," state name of predecessor, type of organization, and period of its existence ▶

Date and place of incorporation: December 15,19 9- Washington

A If this election takes effect for the first tax year the corporation exists, enter the earliest of the following: (1) date the corporation first had shareholders, (2) date the corporation first had assets, or (3) date the corporation began doing business. ▶ Jan. 1,19 9-

B Selected tax year: Annual return will be filed for tax year ending (month and day) ▶ December 31
See Instructions before entering your tax year. If the tax year ends any date other than December 31, you must complete Part II or Part IV on back. You may want to complete Part III to make a back-up request.

C Name of each shareholder, person having a community property interest in the corporation's stock, and each tenant in common, joint tenant, and tenant by the entirety. (A husband and wife (and their estates) are counted as one shareholder in determining the number of shareholders without regard to the manner in which the stock is owned.)	D Shareholders' Consent Statement. We the undersigned shareholders, consent to the corporation's election to be treated as an "S corporation" under section 1362(a). *(Shareholders sign and date below.)	E Stock owned: Number of shares	E Stock owned: Dates acquired	F Social security number (employer identification number for estate or trust)	G Tax year ends (Month and day)
John Doe	John Doe	250	1/1/9-	123-45-6789	12/31
Joe Doe	Joe Doe	250	1/1/9-	987-65-4321	12/31

For this election to be valid, the consent of each shareholder, person having a community property interest in the corporation's stock, and each tenant in common, joint tenant, and tenant by the entirety must either appear above or be attached to this form. (See instructions for column D, if continuation sheet or a separate consent statement is needed.)

Under penalties of perjury, I declare that I have examined this election, including accompanying schedules, and statements, and to the best of my knowledge and belief it is true, correct, and complete.

Signature and Title of Officer ▶ John Doe, President   Date ▶ 1/5/9-

See Parts II, III, and IV on back.

SAMPLE #4
SUBCHAPTER S RESOLUTIONS

The president suggested that the corporation consider electing to be taxed as a small business corporation under Internal Revenue Code subchapter S. The board then discussed the advantages of such an action and on motion, the following resolutions were adopted:

RESOLVED, that the corporation elects to be taxed under Internal Revenue Code subchapter S as a small business corporation;

RESOLVED FURTHER, that the officers of the corporation are authorized and directed to prepare, execute and file, or cause to be prepared, executed and filed, Internal Revenue Service Form 2553, together with a statement by each shareholder consenting to this election, and to do all other acts that may be required to make this election effective.

unless it is terminated in one of the following ways.

(i) Revocation

An election may be revoked by the consent of shareholders owning more than (50%) of the issued and outstanding shares. The revocation is executed and filed in the same manner as an election.

A revocation is effective for the corporation's taxable year if it is made during the first two and one-half months of that taxable year. The revocation statement may specify another date upon which the revocation is to be effective.

(ii) Termination

Whenever an S corporation fails to maintain the requirements of domestic small business corporation status, the election will be terminated. A corporation's election will also be terminated under certain conditions if it derives excessive passive investment income. Examples of passive investment income are royalties, rents, dividends, interest, and annuities.

c. LOST INVESTMENT — SECTION 1244

Section 1244 of the Internal Revenue Code is aimed at encouraging the investment of risk capital in small corporate ventures. Section 1244 permits a kind of stock insurance where shareholders can claim an ordinary loss treatment of their lost investment if the venture fails. This is more favorable than capital tax loss treatment.

Instead of being limited to a capital tax loss of $30,000 per year, shareholders can take an ordinary tax loss of up to $50,000 in actual loss ($100,000 if a joint return is filed) and deduct it from their earnings.

However, recent changes in the tax laws have decreased the immediate benefits considerably. Many corporate owners still make the decision to elect section 1244 status just in case the tax laws change again.

In other words, the corporation can protect its shareholders by preparing in advance for the consequences of the corporation's failure by qualifying the shares as IRC section 1244 stock.

To qualify, the corporation *must* meet the following requirements:

(a) The corporation must be a small business corporation.

(b) The shareholders must be individuals and not corporations or trusts, although partnerships can qualify under special rules.

(c) The stock must be issued for money or other property. Stock issued for services rendered or to be rendered to, or for the benefit of, the corporation does not qualify.

The shareholder of section 1244 stock can take a *100% ordinary tax loss* rather than a capital loss up to $50,000 in actual loss ($100,000 if filing a joint return) if the following conditions are met:

(a) The shareholders purchased the stock from the corporation and not from other shareholders.

(b) The stock is common stock issued by a domestic corporation.

(c) The limits on how much stock may be sold under this plan are complied with. (The amount of section 1244 stock which may be issued may not exceed $1,000,000.)

Meet with your accountant before you organize your corporation and issue shares to ensure you can qualify under section 1244.

4

INCORPORATION PROCEDURE FOR A WASHINGTON CORPORATION

a. GET A COPY OF THE ACT

Every person proposing to incorporate should have a copy of the Washington Business Corporation Act (RCW Title 23 B). The revised act became effective July 1, 1990. While many acts are difficult to understand, the Business Corporation Act is clearly written, well indexed, and organized.

The following is a general, abbreviated, step-by-step list of the procedures necessary to incorporate a private company in Washington, with an explanation of each step.

b. REQUEST FORMS FROM SECRETARY OF STATE

RCW 23B.01.210 provides that the Secretary of State for Washington may prescribe and furnish some specific forms and other unlisted forms on request. It is best to ask the Secretary of State to provide the forms you will need to incorporate to ensure you are using the most recent form available. A kit containing forms necessary for incorporation is available from the publisher. See information on page xi.

c. WHAT'S IN A NAME? — CHOOSING YOUR CORPORATE HANDLE

1. Selecting a name

A company, like a person, must have a name, but unfortunately it is not as easy to pick a name for a company as it is for a new baby. When you select a name for your company, you must consider certain definite factors, the most important one being that the name must be acceptable to the Secretary of State.

The Secretary, however, must have a good and valid reason for not approving a name. In broad terms, any name which is not identical with, or does not closely resemble an existing name, and does not confuse the public is acceptable.

The following is a reprint of sections of the Washington Business Corporation Act which outline the guidelines for an acceptable corporate name.

> **23B.04.010 Corporate name. (Effective July 1, 1990.)** (1) A corporate name:
>
> (a) Must contain the word "corporation," "incorporated," "company," or "limited," or the abbreviated "corp.," " inc.," "co.," or "ltd.;"
>
> (b) Must not contain language stating or implying that the corporation is organized for a purpose other than those permitted by RCW 23B.03.010 and its articles of incorporation;
>
> (c) Must not contain any of the following words or phrases:
>
> "Bank," "banking," "banker," "trust," "cooperative," or any combination of the words "industrial" and "loan," or any combination of any two or more [of the] words "building," "savings," "loan," "home," "association," and "society," or any other words or phrases prohibited by any statute of this state; and
>
> (d) Except as authorized by subsections (2) and (3) of this section, must

be distinguishable upon the records of the secretary of state from:

(i) The corporate name of a corporation incorporated or authorized to transact business in this state;

(ii) A corporate name reserved or registered under RCW 23B.04.020 or 23B.04.030;

(iii) The fictitious name adopted pursuant to RCW 23B.15.060 by a foreign corporation authorized to transact business in this state because its real name is unavailable;

(iv) The corporate name of a not-for-profit corporation incorporated or authorized to conduct affairs in this state;

(v) The name or reserved name of a foreign or domestic limited partnership formed or registered under chapter 25.08 or 25.10 RCW; and

(vi) The name of any limited liability company organized or registered under chapter 25.15 RCW.

(2) A corporation may apply to the secretary of state for authorization to use a name that is not distinguishable upon the records from one or more of the names described in subsection (1) of this section. The secretary of state shall authorize use of the name applied for if:

(a) The other corporation, holder, or limited partnership consents to the use in writing and files with the secretary of state documents necessary to change its name or the name reserved or registered to a name that is distinguishable upon the records of the secretary of state from the name of the applying corporation; or

(b) The applicant delivers to the secretary of state a certified copy of the final judgment of a court of competent jurisdiction establishing the applicant's right to use the name applied for in this state.

(3) A corporation may use the name, including the fictitious name, of another domestic or foreign corporation that is used in this state if the other corporation is incorporated or authorized to transact business in this state and the proposed user corporation:

(a) Has merged with the other corporation; or

(b) Has been formed by reorganization of the other corporation.

(4) This title does not control the use of assumed business names or "trade names." [1989 c 165 § 37.]

(5) A name shall not be considered distinguishable upon the records of the secretary of state by virtue of:

(a) A variation in the designation, under subsection (1)(a) of this section, used for the same name;

(b) The addition or deletion of an article or conjunction such as "the" or "and" from the same name;

(c) Punctuation, capitalization, or special characters or symbols in the same name; or

(d) Use of abbreviation or the plural form of a word in the same name. [1994 c 211 § 1304.]

With the above guidelines in mind, you should try to choose a distinctive name that accurately describes the type of business you intend to carry on. For example, a name like "Quiggly Cleaners Inc." would be a better name for a dry cleaning company than "Western Enterprises Inc." The word "Western" is one of those words that has been so frequently used that it is no longer distinctive. Other tired words are "Northern," "Pacific," and "Universal." No doubt you can think of countless others. The word "Enterprises" does not accurately describe the business of this particular company. It might be used more accurately in naming an investment company of some sort.

One of the easiest ways to check out existing names is to look in the Yellow Pages for the names of companies already doing business in the area. Trade and corporation directories, which are available in any large library, will help you find other protected names of American organizations.

Generally, you should remember that the most successful proposals are likely to be the following:

(a) A coined word (perhaps a combination of incorporators' names) plus a descriptive word

(b) The full name of an individual (e.g., John Albert Doe Inc.). Be careful, however, using your name as the company name. You may get people telephoning you at home at all hours. If your company goes bankrupt, you will be tarred with the same brush for many years simply because of the name. Finally, if you ever sell out, your name will go with the business and somebody else might run it into the ground, with the same results as if you had gone bankrupt.

(c) The name of an individual combined with a descriptive word (e.g., Doe Explorations Inc.)

(d) The combination of a distinctive geographic name plus a descriptive word (e.g., Mt. Baker Machinery Inc.) provided the company is connected with or operating in that area.

Of course, all proposals must contain the word "corporation," "company," "incorporated," "limited," or an abbreviation of one of these words.

Finally, stay away from the names of companies already in existence (or the common contractions of their names). For example, a name like Xerox Construction Inc. implies that your resources are connected with those of Xerox. This is okay if you can show that it is true. If it is not, you may be found guilty of trying to "steal" the name in a "passing off" action brought by Xerox.

Note: The Secretary may approve a name that is registered as a trademark or corporate name in some other jurisdiction. Approval by the Secretary does not guarantee your right to exclusive use of a name. And you may be subject to certain penalties if your intent was to "steal" someone else's business.

2. Procedure

Submit your name to the Secretary of State for approval, along with a $30 fee for reservation. The address is:

Corporations Division
Office of the Secretary of State
505 E. Union, 2nd Floor
P.O. Box 40234
Olympia, WA 98504-0234

The Secretary will reserve the approved name for 180 days. Thus, you have 180 days from the date of reservation to complete incorporation. If incorporation documents are not filed within that time, someone else may claim the name unless you reapply and pay an additional $30 fee. Sample #5 shows the form necessary for reserving your corporation's name. You must send in one original and one copy of the form.

You don't have to go through a name reservation procedure if you leave your corporation name blank and send in three name choices along with the Articles. The office can do the procedure all at once.

d. THE ARTICLES OF INCORPORATION

The information required to be in the Articles of Incorporation is specified in RCW 23B.02.020. The basic forms necessary to incorporate in the state of Washington are shown on the following pages and include a sample of the Articles of Incorporation (see Sample #6).

The total fee for a for-profit corporation filing the Articles of Incorporation and for being licensed is $175.

The articles state the aggregate number of shares that the corporation shall have authority to issue. If the shares are divided into classes or issued in series, a statement of the relative rights, preferences, and limitations applying to each of the classes must

SAMPLE #5
APPLICATION FOR RESERVATION OF NAME

APPLICATION FOR RESERVATION OF NAME

TRANS	AMOUNT REC'D	DATE REC'D	BY
RES			

RESERVATION IS VALID FOR 180 DAYS:
EXPIRATION DATE:________________

CHECK ENTITY TYPE: SUBMIT FEE INDICATED.

[x] **PROFIT CORPORATION: FILING FEE $30.00**
(Name must contain a corporate designation such as "corporation," "incorporated," "company," or "limited," or an abbreviation thereof.)

[ ] **NONPROFIT CORPORATION: FILING FEE $20.00**
(Name may not contain a corporate designation (listed above), however, designations such as "association," "group," "club,", etc. may be used.)

[ ] **LIMITED PARTNERSHIP: FILING FEE $10.00**
(Name must contain the words "Limited Partnership" or the initials L.P.)

****

(PLEASE PRINT OR TYPE)

The undersigned applicant applies to reserve the following name:

1) J & J Personnel Incorporated

2) ________________

3) ________________

(Please list alternative choices in order of preference.
First name available will be reserved and will be indicated by an ok and initials of reviewer by approved name.)

NAME AND ADDRESS OF APPLICANT:

Jack A. Doe
(Name)

222 B Street
(Address)

Anywhere WA 99999
(City) (State) (Zip)

Dated: January 30, 199-

Jack Doe
(SIGNATURE OF APPLICANT)

IF THE ABOVE NAME RESERVATION IS FOR SOMEONE OTHER THAN THE APPLICANT, PLEASE COMPLETE THIS SECTION WITH CLIENT'S NAME AND ADDRESS.

(Name)

(Address)

(City) (State) (Zip)

PLEASE RETURN
APPLICATION AND APPROPRIATE FEE TO:

OFFICE OF THE SECRETARY OF STATE
CORPORATIONS DIVISION
505 E UNION, 2ND FL
PO BOX 40234
OLYMPIA WA 98504-0234
INFORMATION: (360) 753-7115

SCP-INC-WASH(1-1)96

Note: The original form and a copy of the form must be sent.

be attached to the articles. Keep in mind that the taxation benefits of subchapter S and section 1244 are not available to closely held small corporations if they have different classes of shares.

In addition, the issue of corporate control becomes more complicated when different classes of shares exist. If you plan to incorporate with different classes of shares, you would be wise to consult an attorney to set up the different rights and to make sure you understand how the division of rights will affect the operation of the corporation.

The address of the registered office and the name of the registered agent at this address must be stated in the articles. The registered office and the registered agent provide an identifiable place and person where legal documents may be served and to which the Secretary of State's office may forward materials of concern to the corporation. This means that a street address, not a post office box number, must be given. Typically the registered agent will be a corporate officer at the corporate headquarters or the corporation attorney at his or her law office. If you are doing it yourself, you will be the registered agent.

The articles must state the name and address of each incorporator. You can have a single incorporator, and as with directors, there are no citizenship or residence requirements for incorporators. For convenience, a lawyer often acts as the incorporator. Each incorporator must sign the Articles of Incorporation, and all incorporators must be over the age of 18.

Sample #6 is an example of the Articles of Incorporation.

A new corporation must file an Initial Annual Report (see Sample #7) within 120 days of incorporation. The fee for filing this report is $10. You may get the form from the Office of the Secretary of State.

All checks should be certified and made payable to the Secretary of State. All correspondence and forms should be filed with —

Corporations Division
Office of the Secretary of State
505 E. Union, 2nd Floor
P.O. Box 40234
Olympia, WA 98504-0234
Information: (360) 753-7115

e. FILING THE ARTICLES

When your articles and other incorporation papers are prepared, they should be sent to the Secretary of State with a cover letter and your certified check. Following is a checklist to ensure that you have included all necessary items.

(a) Submit at least two sets of the Articles of Incorporation. One set of the articles (the set which will be retained by the Secretary of State) must be signed in pen and ink by each of the incorporators.

(b) The Initial Annual Report may be submitted with the articles, or within 120 days of incorporation.

(c) Prepare cover letter to accompany documents (see Sample #8).

(d) Prepare certified check payable to the Secretary of State to cover fees.

When you have completed everything correctly, the Secretary of State will issue a Certificate of Incorporation (see Sample #9) and a corporation license (see Sample #10). Allow at least two weeks for your certificate to come from the Secretary of State.

When you receive your Certificate of Incorporation and the certified copy of the articles, insert them under the proper tabs in your minute book.

SAMPLE #6
ARTICLES OF INCORPORATION

Articles of Incorporation

UBI #: ____________________

Phone #: 206-456-7890

Pursuant to RCW 23B.02.020 of the Washington Business Corporation Act, the undersigned do(es) hereby submit these Articles of Incorporation for the purpose of forming a business corporation.

1. The name of the corporation is: J & J Personnel Incorporated

(**Note:** The corporate name, shown above, must contain the word "corporation," "incorporated," "company," or "limited," or the abbreviation "corp.," "inc.," "co.," or "ltd.")

2. The number of shares the corporation is authorized to issue: 50,000
(A minimum of one (1) share must be listed.)

2(a). These shares shall be (check only **one** box):
- ☒ all of one class, designated as common stock;
- ☐ divided into classes or series within a class as provided in the attached schedule, with the information required by RCW 23B.06.010 and RCW 23B.06.020.

3. The name of the initial registered agent is: John Doe
(**Note:** The registered agent, appointed above, must reside in the State of Washington *and* sign the consent to appointment as registered agent at the bottom of the page.)

3(a). The initial registered office of the corporation, which address is identical to the business
office of the registered agent in Washington, is:
Number and street: 123 Incorporator Road
City: Seattle, WA Zip code: 99999

3(b). (Optional) The post office box address, **located in the same city as the Washington registered office address**, which may be used for mailing purposes only, is:
P.O. Box #: 123 City: Seattle, WA Zip code: 99999
(**Note:** Include city and zip code above.)

4. **CONSENT TO APPOINTMENT AS REGISTERED AGENT**
(**Note:** Must be completed and signed by person shown as registered agent on line 3.)

I, John Doe, hereby consent to serve as registered agent in the State of Washington for the above-named corporation. I understand that as agent for the corporation, it will be my responsibility to accept service of process on behalf of the corporation; to forward license renewals and other mail to the corporation; and to immediately notify the Office of the Secretary of State in the event of my resignation or of any changes in the registered office address.

John Doe	John Doe President	May 20, 199-
Signature of registered agent	*Print name and title*	*Date*

SCP-INC-WASH(2-1)96

SAMPLE #6 — Continued

5. Any other provisions the corporation elects to include are attached.

6. The name and address of each incorporator is:
(**Note:** A minimum of one incorporator is required.)

Name	Address	City	State	Zip code
John Doe	111 A Street	Seattle	WA	99999

(Attach additional pages if necessary.)

7. These Articles will be effective upon filing, unless an extended date and/or time appears here:
_______________________________, 19____
(**Note:** Extended effective date may be set at not more than 90 days beyond the date the document is stamped "Filed" by the Secretary of State.)

8. The document is hereby executed under penalties of perjury, and is, to the best of my knowledge, true and correct.

Dated: May 20, 19 9-

John Doe
(Signature of Incorporator)

John Doe, Incorporator
(Type or print name)

____
(Signature of Incorporator)

_______________, Incorporator
(Type or print name)

____
(Signature of Incorporator)

_______________, Incorporator
(Type or print name)

____
(Signature of Incorporator)

_______________, Incorporator
(Type or print name)

SCP-INC-WASH(2-2)96

SAMPLE #7
INITIAL ANNUAL REPORT

SECRETARY of STATE

DEPARTMENTAL USE ONLY						
ITEM AND DATE		CORP. NUMBER		CORP. ALPHA		
TRANS CODE	CR TYPE	PAYMENT AMOUNT	TYPE	MULT	REC BY	
LOF	REG	$ 5 00				

INITIAL ANNUAL REPORT FILING FEE **$10.00**

NAME OF CORPORATION: J & J PERSONNEL INCORPORATED

STATE OR COUNTRY OF INCORPORATION: Washington

REGISTEREDOFFICE ADDRESS IN WASHINGTON: 123 Incorporator Road, Seattle, WA 99999

(street and number or rural route and box number including P.O. Box)

(city, state and zip code)

REGISTERED AGENT IN WASHINGTON AT ABOVE ADDRESS: John Doe

BRIEF DESCRIPTION OF THE BUSINESS, IF ANY, WHICH THE CORPORATION INTENDS TO CONDUCT IN WASHINGTON: operation of a personnel agency

ADDRESS OF THE PRINCIPAL PLACE OF BUSINESS OF THE CORPORATION IN WASHINGTON:
123 Incorporator Road, Seattle, WA 99999

ADDRESS OF THE PRINCIPAL PLACE OF BUSINESS OF THE CORPORATION IN THE STATE OF INCORPORATION:

NAMES AND RESPECTIVE ADDRESSES OF OFFICERS & DIRECTORS OF THE CORPORATION (indicate titles):

John Doe, 111 A Street, Seattle, Washington 99999

Jack Doe, 222 B Street, Seattle, Washington 99999

(attach a separate sheet if necessary)

This form shall be executed by an officer or director of the corporation except that the initial report of a domestic corporation may be executed by an incorporator.

John Doe President April 26, 199-

(signature and title of person preparing report) (date)

SUBMIT WITH APPLICATION FOR CERTIFICATE OF AUTHORITY
OR ARTICLES OF INCORPORATION

ssf 26

SAMPLE #8
LETTER TO SECRETARY OF STATE

Corporations Division
Office of the Secretary of State
505 E. Union, 2nd Floor
P.O. Box 40234
Olympia, WA 98504-0234

Re: Incorporation of J & J PERSONNEL INCORPORATED

Dear Secretary:

Enclosed are the following:

(1) One executed original and one copy of Articles of Incorporation with Consent to Serve as Registered Agent

(2) Original and one copy of Initial Annual Report

(3) Check in the amount of one hundred and eighty-five ($185.00) dollars to cover our fees.*

Would you please attend to the incorporation of the above-mentioned company and return a certified copy of the articles to us as soon as possible.

Sincerely,

John Doe

*$175 for incorporation fees and $10 for Initial Annual Report.

SAMPLE #9
CERTIFICATE OF INCORPORATION

STATE of WASHINGTON SECRETARY of STATE

I, Ralph Munro, Secretary of State of the State of Washington and custodian of its seal, hereby issue this

CERTIFICATE OF INCORPORATION

to

J & J PERSONNEL INCORPORATED

a Washington PROFIT corporation. Articles of Incorporation were filed for record in this office on the date indicated below.

VOID

Corporation Number: 29999802 Date: 05-12-199-

Given under my hand and the seal of the State of Washington, at Olympia, the State Capitol.

Ralph Munro, Secretary of State

SSF 57

SAMPLE #10
CORPORATION LICENSE

SSF 47 (4-81)

STATE OF WASHINGTON **SECRETARY OF STATE**

OLYMPIA, WASHINGTON 98504

CORPORATION LICENSE

This certifies that the Corporation named hereon is licensed to do business in the State of Washington.

LICENSE NO. 0123456789

EXPIRATION DATE 05-31-199-

J & J Personnel Incorporated
123 Incorporator Road
Seattle, Washington 99999

RALPH MUNRO
SECRETARY OF STATE

SSF 47 (4-81)

5

POST-INCORPORATION PROCEDURES

Once you have received your Certificate of Incorporation, congratulate yourself. You did it yourself, and saved your new corporation money.

When you have received confirmation of incorporation from the Secretary of State, there are certain post-incorporation procedures you have to take care of. These consist of purchasing a minute book, holding an organizational meeting of directors, issuing shares, opening a bank account for the company, and getting the company's books into shape.

Before you start these procedures, it would be a good idea to look at the general powers of a corporation as defined by the Washington Business Corporation Act.

> **23B.03.020 General powers.** (1) Unless its Articles of Incorporation provide otherwise, every corporation has perpetual duration and succession in its corporate name.
>
> (2) Unless its articles of incorporation provide otherwise, every corporation has the same powers as an individual to do all things necessary or convenient to carry out its business and affairs, including without limitation, power:
>
> (a) To sue and be sued, complain, and defend in its corporate name;
>
> (b) To have a corporate seal, which may be altered at will, and to use it, or a facsimile of it, by impressing or affixing it or in any other manner reproducing it;
>
> (c) To make and amend bylaws, not inconsistent with its articles of incorporation or with the laws of this state, for managing the business and regulating the affairs of the corporation;
>
> (d) To purchase, receive, lease, or otherwise acquire, and own, hold, improve, use, and otherwise deal with, real or personal property, or any legal or equitable interest in property, wherever located;
>
> (e) To sell, convey, mortgage, pledge, lease, exchange, and otherwise dispose of all or any part of its property;
>
> (f) To purchase, receive, subscribe for, or otherwise acquire; own, hold, vote, use, sell, mortgage, lend, pledge, or otherwise dispose of; and deal in and with shares or other interests in, or obligations of, any person;
>
> (g) To make contracts, incur liabilities, borrow money, issue its notes, bonds, and other obligations, which may be convertible into or include the option to purchase other securities of the corporation, and secure any of its obligations by mortgage or pledge of any of its property, franchises, or income;
>
> (h) To make guarantees respecting the contracts, securities, or obligations of any person; including, but not limited to, any shareholder, affiliated or unaffiliated individual, domestic or foreign corporation, partnership, association, joint venture or trust, if such guarantee may reasonably be expected to benefit, directly or indirectly, the guarantor corporation. As to the enforceability of the guarantee, the decision of the board of directors that the guarantee may be reasonably expected to benefit, directly or indirectly, the guarantor corporation shall be binding in respect to the issue of

benefit to the guarantor corporation;

(i) To lend money, invest and reinvest its funds, and receive and hold real and personal property as security for repayment;

(j) To be a promoter, partner, member, associate, or manager of any partnership, joint venture, trust, or other entity;

(k) To conduct its business, locate offices, and exercise the powers granted by this title within or without this state;

(l) To elect, appoint, or hire officers, employees, and other agents of the corporation, define their duties, fix their compensation, and lend them money and credit;

(m) To fix the compensation of directors, and lend them money and credit;

(n) To pay pensions and establish pension plans, pension trusts, profit sharing plans, share bonus plans, share option plans, and benefit or incentive plans for any or all of its current or former directors, officers, employees, and agents;

(o) To make donations for the public welfare or for charitable, scientific or educational purposes;

(p) To transact any lawful business that will aid governmental policy; and

(q) To make payments or donations, or do any other act, not inconsistent with law, that furthers the business and affairs of the corporation. [1989 c 165 § 34.]

a. PURCHASE YOUR MINUTE BOOK

A Washington corporation is required by law to keep minutes of all shareholders' and directors' meetings and other important corporate documents in the registered office or principal place of business. For convenience, most corporations keep minutes and documents like the Certificate of Incorporation, the articles, and the bylaws, as well as shareholder agreements, in what is called a minute book.

This is simply a binder that contains all of the above documents in a neat and orderly fashion. Its major use is as a record place for shareholders' names, addresses, and number of shares held. It is recommended that you get one, as then you will have all of the corporation documents together. (**Note:** In the past, share issues were represented by share certificates. Washington no longer requires share certificates.)

Strictly speaking, Washington corporations do not require a seal. If you decide to have one, you may purchase it from the publisher, as indicated in the front of this book.

b. MAKE YOUR BANKING ARRANGEMENTS

A corporation must have its own bank account and deposit, withdrawal, and checking arrangements, etc., because it is a separate legal entity. These arrangements should be made soon after incorporation by the directors.

The bank you choose to deal with will provide you with the resolution forms necessary to open an account. Occasionally, the bank will ask to see your articles or bylaws to ascertain the extent of corporate borrowing powers. Do not be surprised by this request.

c. HOLD A DIRECTORS' MEETING

Unless you dispense with the Board of Directors (see 23B.08.010(3)), the first meeting of directors is designed to launch the corporation into business, issue shares, elect officers, appoint the corporation's banker, authorize the transfer of assets into the corporation, and make certain tax elections. Remember that it is the directors who sit in power and who theoretically (actually, in most close corporations) direct

SAMPLE #11
FORMAL NOTICE OF ORGANIZATIONAL MEETING

NOTICE OF ORGANIZATIONAL MEETING
OF BOARD OF DIRECTORS
OF
J & J Personnel Inc.

John Doe

Jack Doe

The undersigned, being the incorporator of the corporation, hereby gives the above named initial directors of the corporation notice of the organizational meeting of the Board of Directors of the corporation to be held at *123 Incorporation Road* on the *10th* day of *May, 199-.*

EXECUTED and mailed this *26th day of April, 199-.*

John Doe
____

the corporation on all important issues. Sample #11 is an example of a formal notice of a meeting. However, you could, instead of sending this notice, add the following waiver of notice to the minutes of your meeting.

> Notice is hereby waived by the undersigned directors.

Whenever an important issue arises, it is resolved by the directors and is confirmed by the directors and the minutes of directors. Sample #12 shows the minutes of an actual meeting of directors. In most small close corporations these meetings are merely a formality and it is quite common to consent in writing to the standard items of procedure, and file that consent in lieu of holding an actual meeting. Sample #13 is an illustration of typical consent resolutions in lieu of the organizational meeting of directors. It is included in the package of forms available from the publisher of this book. Sample #14 is a resolution giving corporate officers authority to execute bank resolutions dealing with corporate banking matters.

A subchapter S election or section 1244 stock issuance should be made at this meeting. Section 1244 elections are illustrated in Samples #12 and #13. Subchapter

SAMPLE #12
MINUTES OF ORGANIZATIONAL MEETING

MINUTES OF ORGANIZATIONAL MEETING
OF BOARD OF DIRECTORS
OF

J & J Personnel Inc.

TIME AND PLACE: The organizational meeting of the Board of Directors named in the Articles of Incorporation of: *J & J Personnel Inc.* was held at *123 Incorporation Road, Seattle, Washington* at *9:00 a.m.*, on the *10th* day of *May, 199-*, pursuant to a Waiver of Notice signed by each of the Directors.

PRESENT: *John Doe* presided over the meeting and appointed *Jack Doe* to act as Secretary of the meeting. Also present were:

The Waiver of Notice was presented to the meeting and was ordered filed with the minutes of the meeting.

ARTICLES OF INCORPORATION: The Chairman reported that the Corporation's Articles of Incorporation had been filed in the office of the Secretary of State of the State of Washington, on the *15th* day of *April, 199-*, and that a duplicate counterpart of the Articles of Incorporation, bearing the approval of the Secretary of State of Washington and having attached the Certificate of Incorporation, was presented to the meeting, and the Secretary was instructed to place the copy of the articles and the Certificate of Incorporation in the minute book of the Corporation.

BYLAWS: A set of proposed Bylaws for the regulation and government of the affairs of the Corporation was presented to the meeting. After discussion, and upon motion duly made and seconded, the following resolution was unanimously adopted:

> **RESOLVED:** That the Bylaws in the form presented to this meeting are hereby approved and adopted as the Bylaws of the Corporation and that the Secretary is directed to file them in the minute book.

*** ELECTION OF OFFICERS:** The meeting was declared open for election of officers. After discussion, upon motion duly made and seconded, the following officers were unanimously elected to serve until the next annual meeting and until their respective successors are elected and qualified:

PRESIDENT: *John Doe*
SECRETARY-TREASURER: *Jack Doe*

* **Note:** Only the President and Secretary are necessary. In a one-person company, the shareholder has both positions.

SAMPLE #12 — Continued

***SECTION 1244 PLAN:** The Board of Directors next considered the desirability of stock insurance as a small business corporation under Section 1244 of the Internal Revenue Code, which under certain circumstances permits individual subscribing shareholders to take ordinary rather than capital losses if they sell their stock at a loss or if the Corporation is dissolved and they suffer a loss. After discussion, and upon motion duly made and seconded, the following resolution was unanimously adopted:

> **RESOLVED:** That the Stock Issuance in the form presented to this meeting is hereby approved and adopted by the Corporation.

SUBSCRIPTION OF STOCK OF COMPANY: After discussion, upon motion duly made and seconded, the following resolution was unanimously adopted:

> **RESOLVED:** That the subscriptions of each of the following persons for the number of shares set forth opposite their name are accepted and upon payment to the Corporation of the amount set forth opposite a subscriber's name.

NAME	SHARES	PURCHASE PRICE
John Doe	*250 common shares*	*$250 (two hundred fifty)*
Jack Doe	*250 common shares*	*$250 (two hundred fifty)*

PAID IN CAPITAL: The subscribers then each delivered their check in the amount specified above to the Corporation.

The Chairman announced that the Corporation had now received consideration of a value of at least $500 for the issuance of shares as required by the Articles of Incorporation and the Corporation is now authorized to transact business.

BANK ACCOUNT: It was considered advisable for the Corporation to establish a bank account with the *Anywhere* Branch of *Savings Bank of Washington*. The bank's resolution form being presented to the meeting and, on motion duly made and seconded, the resolution incorporated therein was unanimously adopted. Two copies of the form were then executed and the Secretary was directed to deliver one copy to the bank and to file the other copy with the minutes of this meeting.

There being no further business to come before this meeting, the meeting was adjourned.

Jack Doe

SECRETARY

ATTEST:

John Doe

*Note: Optional. Before including this clause, see chapter 3 on section 1244.

SAMPLE #13
CONSENT RESOLUTIONS IN LIEU OF ORGANIZATIONAL MEETING OF DIRECTORS

Consent to Action of Board of Directors in Lieu of Organizational Meeting of Directors of

J&J Personnel Inc.

The undersigned, being all of the initial Board of Directors of this corporation, consent to the following actions of the Board of Directors.

1. The undersigned consent to the filing of the Articles of Incorporation with the Certificate of Incorporation in the minute book of the corporation.

2. The bylaws attached hereto and incorporated by this reference are hereby adopted as the bylaws of this corporation.

3. The following are hereby elected as officers of the corporation to serve until their successors are elected and qualified.

President	John Doe
* Vice-President	
Secretary	Jack Doe
* Treasurer	

4.** It is deemed desirable that the offer, sale, and issuance of the corporation's stock be effectuated in such a manner that the qualified shareholders may receive the benefits of Section 1244 of the Internal Revenue Code and therefore the following plan to issue Section 1244 stock is hereby adopted by the Board of Directors:

(a) The plan as herein set forth shall be effective immediately.

(b) The corporation is authorized to offer and to issue 1,000 shares of common stock with a par value of $1(one dollar) per share, and all of such stock shall be issued subsequent to the date the plan becomes effective and for a period not to exceed two years from the date of adoption of the plan, or to the date when the corporation shall make a subsequent offering of any stock, whichever date shall occur first.

(c) During the period set forth in paragraph (b) above, the corporation shall offer and issue only such common stock.

(d) The maximum amount to be received by the corporation in consideration of the stock to be issued pursuant to this plan shall be $500,000.

(e) Such common stock shall be issued only for money or other property, provided such other property shall not be stock or securities.

(f) Such other action shall be taken by the corporation as shall qualify the stock offered and issued under this plan as "Section 1244 stock" as such term is defined in the Internal Revenue Code and the regulations issued thereunder, and the officers of the corporation are hereby authorized, empowered, and directed to do and perform any and all acts and deeds necessary to carry out such plan.

* *Note: Only the President and Secretary are necessary.*

** *No. 4 is optional. Delete if not applicable to you.*

SAMPLE #13 — Continued

5. The subscriptions of each of the following persons for the number of shares set forth opposite his or her name are accepted.

NAME	SHARES	PURCHASE PRICE
Jack Doe	250	$250 (two hundred fifty)
John Doe	250	$250 (two hundred fifty)

6. As the subscribers have delivered their checks for the specified amounts to the corporation, the undersigned agree that the corporation has now received consideration of a value of at least $500.00 for the issuance of shares as required by the Articles of Incorporation and is now authorized to transact business.

7. The resolutions attached hereto and incorporated by this reference establishing the banks for the deposit of the corporation's funds are hereby unanimously adopted.

APPROVED and CONSENTED to as of May 10, 199-
(date)

John Doe John Doe

Jack Doe Jack Doe

____

____

____

____

(Directors sign here)

SAMPLE #14
BANKING RESOLUTION

RESOLVED, that the President and the Secretary-Treasurer of the corporation, are hereby authorized to execute on behalf of the corporation any and all forms of bank resolutions dealing with corporate banking matters, including the establishing and maintaining of corporate bank accounts, which in their judgment from time to time may be required for the proper fiscal management of the corporation, including the designation thereon of such authorized signatures of corporate officers as may to them seem appropriate. The said officers may execute such banking resolution or resolutions as if authorized to do so by a specific resolution of the Board of Directors adopted on the date this resolution was adopted by the board.

DATED *May 10, 199-*

John Doe
____
John Doe

Jack Doe
____
Jack Doe

S election may be found in the minutes for a subchapter S election illustrated in chapter 3, Sample #4. Also remember to file Form 2553 for subchapter S election with IRS. Because future tax complications can result if these elections are made by companies whose growth and expansion makes them unsuitable for this type of tax treatment, it is advisable to obtain advice from an accountant experienced in corporate taxation before making either or both of these elections.

d. ADOPT THE BYLAWS

When you read the sample minutes of the organizational meeting of directors or the consent resolutions in lieu of the organizational meeting, you will see a clause or resolution adopting bylaws. All Washington corporations need bylaws to govern the internal workings of the corporation.

The Business Corporation Act does not specify a certain form or terms to be included in bylaws, but remember that your bylaws will be used by corporate officers and directors to determine the requirements for notices, meetings, duties of officers, and other matters which may arise from time to time. Therefore, it is not necessarily a wasteful duplication to include in the bylaws some of the matters which are covered by statute or by the Articles of Incorporation.

In addition, because the bylaws can be more easily changed than the Articles of Incorporation, it is better to have all foreseeable contingencies covered in them. Sample #15 shows a set of bylaws that cover the important aspects of running a small business corporation. This is the set that is available from the publisher and described in the front of the book.

SAMPLE #15
BYLAWS

Bylaws
of

J & J Personnel Inc.

ARTICLE 1 (Offices)

The principal office of the corporation shall be located at: 111 A Street, Anywhere, Washington.

The corporation may have such other offices, either within or without the State of Washington, as the Board of Directors ("Board") may designate or as the business of the corporation may require from time to time.

ARTICLE 2 (Shareholders)

2.1. **Annual Meeting:** The annual meeting of the shareholders shall be held the first week of January in each year at the office of the corporation for the purpose of electing directors and transacting such other business as may come before the meeting. If the day fixed for the annual meeting is a legal holiday at the place of the meeting, the meeting shall be held on the next succeeding business day. If the election of directors is not held on the day designated for the annual meeting of the shareholders, or at any adjournment thereof, the election shall be held at a special meeting of the shareholders called as soon thereafter as practicable.

2.2. **Special Meetings:** The President or the Board may call special meetings of the shareholders for any purpose. At the request of the holders of not less than one-tenth of all of the outstanding shares of the corporation entitled to vote at the meeting, the President shall call a special meeting of the shareholders.

2.3. **Place of Meeting:** All meetings shall be held at the principal office of the corporation or at such other place within or without the State of Washington designated by the Board or by a waiver of notice signed by all of the shareholders entitled to vote at the meeting.

2.4. **Notice of Meeting:** The President or Board when calling an annual or special meeting of shareholders shall cause to be delivered to each shareholder entitled to vote at the meeting either personally or by mail not less than 10 nor more than 50 days before the meeting written notice stating the place, day and hour of the meeting and, in the case of a special meeting, the purpose or purposes of which the meeting is called.

2.5. **Action by Shareholders Without a Meeting:** Any action required or permitted to be taken at a shareholders' meeting may be taken without a meeting if a written consent setting forth the action so taken is signed by all shareholders entitled to vote with respect to the subject matter thereof. Any such consent shall be inserted in the minute book as if it were the minutes of a shareholders' meeting.

2.6. **Quorum:** A majority of the outstanding shares of the corporation entitled to vote, represented in person or by proxy, shall constitute a quorum at a shareholders' meeting. If less than a majority of the outstanding shares are represented at a meeting, a majority of the shares so represented may adjourn the meeting from time to time without further notice. At an adjourned meeting at which a quorum is present or represented, any business may be transacted that might have been transacted at the meeting as originally notified. The shareholders present at a duly organized meeting may continue to transact business until adjournment, notwithstanding the withdrawal of enough shareholders to leave less than a quorum.

2.7. **Proxies:** At all shareholders' meetings a shareholder may vote by proxy executed in writing by the shareholder or by his attorney in fact. Such proxy shall be filed with the Secretary of the corporation before or at the time the meeting. Unless otherwise provided in the proxy, a proxy shall be invalid after 11 months from the date of its execution.

2.8. **Voting of Shares:** Each outstanding share entitled to vote shall be entitled to one vote upon each matter submitted to a vote at a meeting of shareholders.

2.9. **Cumulative Voting:** Each shareholder entitled to vote at an election of directors may vote in person or by proxy the number of shares owned by him for as many persons as there are directors to be elected and for whose election he has a right to vote or he may cumulate his votes by distributing among one or more candidates as many votes as are equal to the number of such directors multiplied by the number of his shares.

Optional. Delete if not applicable.

ARTICLE 3 (Board of Directors)

3.1. **General Powers:** The business and affairs of the corporation shall be managed by the Board.

Insert the number you choose.

3.2. **Number, Tenure and Qualifications:** The Board shall be composed of 2 (two) directors, provided, however, that the number of directors may be changed from time to time to any number. If at any time the number of directors is less than three, the number of directors shall equal the number of shareholders. No decrease in the number of directors shall have the effect of shortening the term of any incumbent director. Each director shall hold office until the next annual meeting until his successor shall have been elected and qualifies unless he resigns or is removed. Directors need not be shareholders of the corporation.

3.3. **Regular Meetings:** A regular Board meeting shall be held without notice immediately after and at the same place as the annual meeting of shareholders. By resolution, the Board may provide the time and place either within or without the State of Washington for holding additional regular meetings without other notice than such resolution.

3.4. **Special Meetings:** Special Board meetings may be called by or at the request of the President or any two directors. The person or persons authorized to call special meetings may fix any place either within or without the State of Washington as the place for holding any special Board meeting called by them.

3.5. **Notice:** Written notice of each special Board meeting shall be delivered personally, telegraphed or mailed to each director at his business address at least two days before the meeting. If such notice is mailed, it shall be deemed to be delivered when deposited in the United States mail properly addressed, with postage prepaid. If the notice is telegraphed, it shall be deemed to be delivered when the content of the telegram is delivered to the telegraph office. The attendance of a director at a meeting shall constitute a waiver of notice of such meeting, except where a director attends a meeting for the express purpose of objecting to the transaction of any business because the meeting is not lawfully called or convened. Neither the business to be transacted at, nor the purpose of, any regular or special meeting of the Board need be specified in the notice or waiver of notice of such meeting.

3.6. **Quorum:** A majority of the directors shall constitute a quorum for the transaction of business at any Board meeting but, if less than such majority be present at a meeting, a majority of the directors present may adjourn the meeting from time to time without further notice.

3.7. **Manner of Acting:** The act of the majority of the directors present at a meeting at which a quorum is present shall be the act of the Board.

3.8. **Vacancies:** Any vacancy occurring on the Board may be filled by the affirmative vote of a majority of the remaining directors though less than a quorum of the Board. A director elected to fill a vacancy shall be elected for the unexpired term of his predecessor in office. Any directorship to be filled by reason of an increase in the number of directors shall be filled by election at an annual meeting or at a special shareholders' meeting called for that purpose.

3.9. **Removal:** At a meeting of shareholders called expressly for that purpose, one or more members of the Board (including the entire Board) may be removed, with or without cause, by a vote of the holders of a majority of the shares then entitled to vote on election of directors. (If less than the entire Board is to be removed, no one of the directors may be removed if the votes cast against his removal would be sufficient to elect him if then cumulatively voted at an election of the entire Board.)

3.10. **Compensation:** By Board resolution, directors may be paid their expenses, if any, of attendance at each Board meeting or a fixed sum for attendance at each Board meeting or a stated salary as director or any combination of the foregoing. No such payment shall preclude any director from serving the corporation in any other capacity and receiving compensation therefor.

3.11. **Presumption of Assent:** A director of the corporation present at a Board meeting at which action on any corporate matter is taken shall be presumed to have assented to the action taken unless his dissent is entered in the minutes of the meeting or unless he files his written dissent to such action with the person acting as the Secretary of the meeting before the adjournment thereof or unless he forwards such dissent by registered mail to the Secretary of the corporation immediately after the adjournment of the meeting. A director who voted in favor of such action may not dissent.

3.12. **Action by Directors without a Meeting:** Any action required or permitted to be taken at a meeting of the Board may be taken without a meeting if a written consent setting forth the action to be taken is signed by each of the directors. Any such written consent shall be inserted in the minute book as if it were the minutes of a Board meeting.

ARTICLE 4 (Officers)

Delete inapplicable positions. President and Secretary are necessary.

4.1. **Number:** The officers of the corporation shall be a President, one or more Vice-Presidents, a Secretary and a Treasurer, each of whom shall be elected by the Board. Such other officers and assistant officers as may be deemed necessary may be elected or appointed by the Board. Any two or more offices may be held by the same person, except the offices of President and Secretary provided that if there is only one shareholder/director, then he may be both President and Secretary.

4.2. **Election and Term of Office:** The officers of the corporation shall be elected annually by the Board at the Board meeting held after the annual meeting of the shareholders. If the election of officers is not held at such meeting, such election shall be held as soon thereafter as a Board meeting conveniently may be held. Each officer shall hold office until the next annual meeting and until his successor shall have been elected and qualified unless he resigns or is removed.

4.3. **Vacancies:** A vacancy in any office because of death, resignation, removal, disqualification or otherwise, may be filled by the Board for the unexpired portion of the term.

4.5. **President:** The President shall be the principal executive officer of the corporation and, subject to the Board's control, shall supervise and control all of the business and affairs of the corporation. When present, he shall preside over all shareholders' meetings and over all Board meetings. With the Secretary or other officer of the corporation authorized by the Board, he may sign certificates for shares of the corporation, deeds, mortgages, bonds, contract, or other instruments that the Board has authorized to be executed, except when the signing and execution thereof has been expressly delegated by the Board or by these Bylaws to some other officer or agent of the corporation or is required by law to be otherwise signed or executed by some other officer or in some other manner. In general, he shall perform all duties incident to the office of President and such other duties as may be prescribed by the Board from time to time.

4.6. **Vice-President:** In the absence of the President or in the event of his death, inability or refusal to act, the Vice-President (or in the event of more than one Vice-President, the Vice-President who was first elected to such office) shall perform the duties of the President, and when so acting, shall have all the powers of and be subject to all the restrictions upon the President. Vice-Presidents shall perform such other duties as from time to time may be assigned to them by the President or by the Board.

Note: Seal is not mandatory in Washington.

4.7. **Secretary:** The Secretary shall: (a) keep the minutes of shareholders' and Board meetings in one or more books provided for that purpose; (b) see that all notices are duly given in accordance with the provisions of these Bylaws or as required by law; (c) be custodian of the corporate records and of the seal of the corporation and see that the seal of the corporation is affixed to all documents, the execution of which on behalf of the corporation under its seal is duly authorized; (d) keep a register of the post office address of each shareholder as furnished to the Secretary by each shareholder; (e) sign with the President, or Vice-President certificates for shares of the corporation, the issuance of which has been authorized by resolution of the Board; (f) have general charge of the stock transfer books of the corporation; and (g) in general perform all duties incident to the office of Secretary and such other duties as from time to time may be assigned to him by the President or by the Board.

4.8. **Treasurer:** If required by the Board, the Treasurer shall give a bond for the faithful discharge of his duties in such sum and with such surety or sureties as the Board shall determine. He shall have charge and custody of and be responsible for all funds and securities of the corporation; receive and give receipts for moneys due and payable to the corporation from any source whatsoever, and deposit all such moneys in the name of the corporation in such banks, trust companies or other depositaries as shall be selected in accordance with the provisions of these Bylaws and in general perform all of the duties incident to the office of Treasurer and such other duties as from time to time may be assigned to him by the President or by the Board.

4.9. **Salaries:** The salaries of the officers shall be fixed from time to time by the Board, and no officer shall be prevented from receiving such salary by reason of the fact that he is also a director of the corporation.

ARTICLE 5 (Contracts, Loans, Checks and Deposits)

5.1. **Contracts:** The Board may authorize any officer or officers, agent or agents, to enter into any contract or execute and deliver any instrument in the name of and on behalf of the corporation, and such authority may be general or confined to specific instances.

5.2. **Loans:** No loans shall be contracted on behalf of the corporation and no evidences of indebtedness shall be issued in its name unless authorized by a resolution of the Board. Such authority may be general or confined to specific instances.

5.3. **Loans to Officers and Directors:** No loans shall be made by the corporation to its officers or directors, unless first approved by the holders of two-thirds of the shares, and no loans shall be made by the corporation secured by its shares.

5.4. **Checks, drafts, etc.:** All checks, drafts or other orders for the payment of money, notes or other evidences of indebtedness issued in the name of the corporation, shall be signed by such officer or officers, agent or agents, of the corporation and in such manner as from time to time determined by resolution of the Board.

5.5. **Deposits:** All funds of the corporation not otherwise employed shall be deposited from time to time to the credit of the corporation in such banks, trust companies or other depositaries as the Board may select.

ARTICLE 6 (Transfer of Shares)

6.1. **Transfer of Shares:** Transfer of shares of the corporation shall be made only on the stock transfer books of the corporation by the holder of record thereof or his legal representative, who shall furnish proper evidence of authority to transfer, or by his attorney in fact authorized by power of attorney duly executed and filed with the Secretary of the corporation. The person in whose name shares stand on the books of the corporation shall be deemed by the corporation to be the owner thereof for all purposes.

6.2. **Share Transfer Restriction.** No shareholder shall sell or otherwise dispose of any of the shares in the corporation, now or hereafter acquired by him, except under the following terms and conditions:

(a) A person (herein called the "proposing transferor") desiring to transfer any share or shares in the corporation shall give notice in writing (herein called "transfer notice") to the corporation that he desires to transfer the same. The transfer notice shall specify the price, which shall be expressed in lawful money of the United States and the terms of payment upon which the proposing transferor is prepared to transfer the share or shares and shall constitute the corporation his agent for the sale thereof to any shareholder or shareholders of the corporation at the price and upon the terms of payment so specified. The transfer notice shall also state whether or not the proposing transferor has had an offer to purchase the shares or any of them from, or proposes to sell the shares or any of them to, any particular person or persons who are not shareholders, and if so the names and addresses of such persons shall be specified in the transfer notice. The transfer notice shall constitute an offer by the proposing transferor to the other shareholder of the corporation holding shares of the class or classes included in the transfer notice and shall not be revocable except with the sanction of the directors. If the transfer notice pertains to shares of more than one class then the consideration and terms of payment for each class of shares shall be stated separately in the transfer notice.

(b) The directors shall forthwith upon receipt thereof transmit the transfer notice to each of the shareholders, other than the proposing transferor, holding shares of the class or classes set forth in the transfer notice and request the shareholder to whom the transfer notice is sent to state in writing within 14 days from the date of the transfer notice whether he is willing to accept any, and if so, the maximum number of shares he is willing to accept at the price and upon the terms specified in the transfer notice. A shareholder shall only be entitled to purchase shares of the class or classes held by him.

(c) Upon the expiration of the 14-day notice period referred to in article 6.2(b), if the directors shall have received from the shareholders entitled to receive the transfer notice sufficient acceptances to take up the full number of shares offered by the transfer notice and, if the transfer notice includes shares of more than one class, sufficient acceptances from the members of each class to take up the full number of shares of each class offered by the transfer notice, the directors shall thereupon apportion shares so offered among the shareholders so accepting and so far as may be, pro rata, according to the number of shares held by each of them respectively, and in the case of more than one class of shares, then pro rata in respect of each class. If the directors shall not have received sufficient acceptances as aforesaid, they may, but only with the consent of the proposing transferor who shall not be obliged to sell to shareholders in the aggregate less than the total number of shares of one or more classes of shares offered by the transfer notice, apportion the shares so offered among the shareholders so accepting so far as may be according to the number of shares held by each respectively but only up to the amount accepted by such shareholders respectively. Upon any such apportionment being made, the proposing transferor shall be bound upon payment of the price to transfer the shares to the respective shareholders to whom the directors have apportioned same. If, in any case, the proposing transferor, having become so bound fails in transferring any share, the corporation may receive the purchase money for that share and shall upon receipt cause the name of the purchasing shareholders to be entered in the register as the holder of the shares and cancel the certificate of the share held by the proposed transferor, whether the same shall be produced to the corporation or not, and shall hold such purchase money

4

corporation may receive the purchase money for that share and shall upon receipt cause the name of the purchasing shareholders to be entered in the register as the holder of the shares and cancel the certificate of the share held by the proposed transferor, whether the same shall be produced to the corporation or not, and shall hold such purchase money in trust for the proposing transferor. The receipt of the corporation for the purchase money shall be a good discharge to the purchasing shareholders and after his name has been entered in the register the validity of the proceedings shall not be questioned by any person.

(d) In the event that some or all of the shares offered shall not be sold under the preceding articles within the 14-day period referred to in article 6.2(b), the proposing transferor shall be at liberty for a period of 90 days after the expiration of that period to transfer such of the shares so offered as are not sold to any person provided that he shall not sell them at a price less than that specified in the transfer notice or on terms more favorable to a purchaser than those specified in the transfer notice.

(e) The provisions as to transfer contained in this article shall not apply:

(i) if before the proposed transfer of shares is made, the transferor shall obtain consents to the proposed transfer from members of the corporation, who at the time of the transfer are the registered holders of two-thirds or more of the issued shares of the class to be transferred to the corporation or if the shares comprise more than one class, then from the registered holders of two-thirds or more of the shares of each class to be transferred and such consent shall be taken to be a waiver of the application of the preceding articles as regards such transfer; or

(ii) to a transfer of shares desired to be made merely for the purpose of effectuating the appointment of a new trustee for the owner thereof, provided that it is proved to the satisfaction of the Board that such is the case.

(f) Nothing herein shall preclude any shareholder from transferring by gift or devise any shares to spouse or any child or children of the shareholder.

ARTICLE 7 (Fiscal Year)

The fiscal year of the corporation shall be the calendar year.

ARTICLE 8 (Seal)

The Seal of this corporation shall consist of the name of the corporation, the state of its incorporation and the year of its incorporation.

ARTICLE 9 (Waiver of Notice)

Whenever any notice is required to be given to any shareholder or director of the corporation under the provisions of these Bylaws or under the provisions of the Articles of Incorporation or under the provisions of the Washington Business Corporation Act, a waiver thereof in writing, signed by the person or persons entitled to such notice, whether before or after the time stated therein, shall be deemed equivalent to the giving of such notice.

ARTICLE 10 (Indemnification)

To the full extent permitted by the Washington Business Corporation Act the corporation shall indemnify any person who was or is a party or is threatened to be made a party to any civil, criminal, administrative or investigative action, suit or proceeding (whether brought by or in the right of the corporation or otherwise) by reason of the fact that he is or was a director or officer of the corporation, or is or was serving at the request of the corporation as a director or officer of another corporation, against expenses (including attorneys' fees), judgments, fines and liabilities, reasonably incurred by or imposed upon him in connection with or resulting from any claim, action, suit, or proceeding, provided that he acted in good faith and in a manner he reasonably believed to be in or not opposed to the best interests of the corporation. The termination of any action, suit, or proceeding by judgment, order, settlement, or conviction or upon a plea of *nolo contendere* or its equivalent shall not, of itself, create a presumption that the person did not act in good faith and in a manner which he reasonably believed to be in, or not opposed to, the best interests of the corporation. The board of directors may obtain insurance on behalf of any person who is or was a director, officer, employee, or agent against any liability arising out of his status as such, whether or not the corporation would have power to indemnify him against such liability. The Board of Directors may, at any time, approve indemnification under the Washington Business Corporation Act, of any other person which the corporation has the power to indemnify. The indemnification provided by this section shall not be deemed exclusive of any other rights to which a person may be entitled as a matter of law or by contract.

SAMPLE #15 — Continued

ARTICLE 11 (Amendments)

These Bylaws may be altered, amended or repealed and new Bylaws may be adopted by the Board at any regular or special meeting of the Board.

ADOPTED BY THE BOARD OF DIRECTORS this 10th **day of** May **, 19 9-**

John Doe
DIRECTOR

Jack Doe
DIRECTOR

DIRECTOR

e. ISSUE SHARES

The issuing and canceling of shares is a relatively simple affair. You should be careful, however, to distinguish among the initial issue of shares upon incorporation, subsequent issues, and simple transfers of already issued shares from one person to another. All three of these dealings involve different operations. You must be sure to prepare the appropriate directors' minutes confirming the issuance, transfer, or cancellation of shares. (Actually, there should never be a cancellation unless there is, at the same time, a transfer so that two would be incorporated into the same minutes.)

1. Initial issue or allotment of shares

An example of the resolution needed to issue shares out of the treasury can be found in the minutes of the organizational meeting of the Board of Directors (Sample #12).

2. Subsequent issue or allotment of shares

Suppose the directors decide to issue additional shares. Under Washington law, existing shareholders have first chance at the new issue of shares. This first chance is called a *pre-emptive right*. It simply means that the existing shareholders have the right to maintain their *proportionate* positions in relation to the other shareholders on a new issue of shares. For example, J & J Personnel Inc., on the initial issue, allotted 50 shares to John Doe and 50 shares to Jack Doe. If the directors decide to issue a further 200 shares, each shareholder has the right to take up a further 100 shares.

In many cases, because the shareholders and directors are the same persons, all parties agree to a new issue of shares and the pre-emptive regulations are just an extra headache. Theoretically, of course, the pre-emptive rights are a welcome reform measure because, too often in the past, the right to make new issues of shares was effectively used to water down the rights of minority shareholders.

To make sure that existing shareholders can exercise their pre-emptive rights, one of the forms shown in Samples #16 and #17 should be completed and filed in the minute book. Each shareholder must sign a waiver (Sample #16), or must at least receive a Notice of Offer to Allot Shares (Sample #17). (Allotting shares is another way of saying issuing shares.) Any shareholder who does not want to purchase new shares should sign the waiver to evidence refusal.

If the shareholders will not sign waivers, then all shareholders should be given Notices of Offer to Allot Shares.

All shareholders who want to purchase new shares should sign and file a shareholder's acceptance form (see Sample #18).

Finally the minutes of the meeting of directors confirming the issues should be drawn up.

3. Value of shares

Questions often arise over what price the shares should be valued at when a new partner is buying into the company.

Most people I know running small businesses are not about to hire some outside business consultant to "value" the shares. And, as is often the case, the new partner is brought in because of what expertise he or she can contribute to the business and consequently does not pay full market value for the shares.

Under the Internal Revenue Code, if a new shareholder pays less than fair market value for shares, then the balance is called a "taxable benefit" and must be included in the new shareholder's income as a capital gain for the year in which the shares are received.

Obviously, there are problems for the tax department questioning this type of valuation in a small, private company.

However, should the IRS audit your company's return and reassess the person involved (which usually involves a relative or close friend), it is up to the taxpayer to "disprove" the tax department's position — which is also very difficult to do.

There are some legal steps around this problem, — such as claiming a reserve against the "gain," or having the new shareholder purchase an "option" instead of the shares themselves, at a much lower price, — but all of these steps require some assistance from a professional and really go beyond the scope of this book. If this situation applies to you, you will need some expert advice before making any moves.

Note: Employees may buy new shares at any price without being considered to have received a taxable benefit. The only requirement is that the employees keep the shares in their name for two years.

When the shares are sold, the difference between the actual purchase price and the sale price is a capital gain, taxable at one-half.

This tax advantage offers employees the opportunity to buy a substantial interest in their company for very little money and receive a valuable employee benefit.

In Washington, the law also allows the corporation to create and issue options to purchase stock. If the options are not given to existing shareholders generally, then the options must be approved by an affirmative vote of the majority of the shareholders of record. The price cannot be less than par value, if the shares are par value shares.

Your local courthouse or business library should have precedents or guides for you to follow in drawing up an option. Otherwise, your accountant can help. At any rate, notifying shareholders of options to purchase should not be too different from notifying them of allotments. Most small businesses will not become concerned with options until they become well

SAMPLE #16
WAIVER OF RIGHTS

Shareholder of *J & J Personnel Inc.* has waived and hereby waives the right of the undersigned to receive an offer with respect to the allotment of *500 common shares* in the capital of the corporation at a price of *$1 per share* by *Woody B. Stockholder* which is proposed by the directors of the company.

John Doe

SAMPLE #17
NOTICE OF OFFER TO ALLOT SHARES

TO: Shareholders of
J & J Personnel Inc.

TAKE NOTICE that the directors of *J & J Personnel Inc.* propose to allot to *Woody B. Stockholder* of *321 Investor's Avenue, Seattle, Washington*, a total of *1,000 common shares* in the capital of the corporation, or the balance thereof not taken up by the shareholders of the corporation pursuant to the following offer, for subscription price of *$1 per share*, payable in cash on or before allotment.

The directors hereby offer *250 common shares* to the holders of common shares in the capital of the corporation pro rata to their respective holdings of common shares in the company as of the date hereof to the closest number of whole shares, excluding fractions, at a price of *$1 per share*, payable in cash on or before allotment. This offer may be accepted by mailing by prepaid registered post or by delivering to the company at *123 Incorporation Road, Seattle, Washington*, the attached form of acceptance within 14 days of the date of this notice, following which period this offer expires.

established and prosperous, unless unusual circumstances arise.

4. Transfer of shares

This refers to the simple transfer of issued shares from one shareholder to one or more other shareholders or strangers.

Ordinarily, the Articles of Incorporation or the bylaws will set out the method for transferring shares. In general, this simply means that the selling shareholder should notify the secretary or treasurer of the corporation of the transfer of shares and instruct him or her to make note of the transfers in the corporate books and records.

In the case of a corporation which uses the illustrated bylaws (see Sample #15), the sale of shares by a shareholder is specifically restricted. Other agreements between shareholders may also place restrictions on the sale and/or transfer of shares. Such restrictions give shareholders the right of first refusal to purchase the seller's shares and also give the remaining shareholders the right to purchase them on a pro rata basis. If all or some of the shareholders decline to accept the offer, the person offering the shares may —

(a) decline to sell the shares not accepted,

(b) offer the remaining shares to shareholders who accepted the offer in the first instance,

(c) sell the remaining shares to third parties.

Sample #19 shows a suggested form to use in giving notice of sale, if your articles, bylaws, or agreement with other shareholders require giving to the remaining shareholders a right of first refusal.

5. Who takes title to shares?

The name in which you take title to the corporate shares you purchase depends upon your particular circumstances.

SAMPLE #18
SHAREHOLDER'S ACCEPTANCE

The undersigned holder of common shares in *J & J Personnel Inc.* hereby accepts the offer of allotment of common shares set out in the notice at a price and on terms therein set forth to the extent of 250 common shares or the pro rata portion of the undersigned in accordance with the terms of said offer, whichever is the lesser.

DATED: *December 20, 199-*

Jack Doe
Signature of Shareholder

SAMPLE #19
NOTICE OF OFFER TO TRANSFER SHARES

NOTICE TO:

John Doe and *Woody B. Stockholder* and:

TO:

J & J Personnel Inc.

TAKE NOTICE that *Jack Doe* desires to sell *500 common shares* of the corporation for the price of *$2 per share* payable in cash on transfer date.

AND FURTHER TAKE NOTICE that this notice hereby empowers *J & J Personnel Inc.* to be my agent in transfer of said shares to any member or members of the corporation. (See Article 6.2(a) of bylaws.)

AND FURTHER TAKE NOTICE that this notice hereby empowers *J & J Personnel Inc.* in transferring said shares.

DATED: *December 20, 199-*

Jack Doe
Signature of Transferor

(a) If you are unmarried and will own 100% of the shares you purchase, take title to the shares in your name alone. This is your "separate property."

(b) If you are married but are purchasing your shares with money or assets acquired and owned by you prior to marriage (separate property), you may take title in your name alone as your separate property.

(c) If you are married and you purchase your shares with community funds (money earned by either you or your spouse after marriage), you may take title to the shares as holders of community property, as joint tenants in common (meaning each party owns an undivided interest individually).

You may also take title in the name of both you and your spouse as *joint tenants*. Joint tenancy means that upon the death of one spouse, the surviving spouse will automatically become the sole owner and take title to the shares. In this case, the shares are not subject to probate. When shares are purchased with your "separate money" and title is taken by you and your spouse as joint tenants, the shares are considered a gift to your spouse and may be subject to a federal gift tax.

6. Redemption — repurchase of shares by the company

Your company is empowered to redeem shares that have a right of redemption attached to them and to purchase its own shares in accordance with the provisions of the act.

The company must not repurchase or redeem shares when it is insolvent or if such action would cause the company to become insolvent.

If your company is considering the purchase of some of its shares to reduce its capital gain base, you should seek professional advice because of the tax ramifications of such a purchase.

f. TRANSFERRING ASSETS TO THE NEW CORPORATION

1. Advantages and disadvantages

Many people who incorporate believe that a company that owns assets is in a more favored position with regard to tax write-offs (i.e., depreciation and expenses) than an individual. This is not necessarily true.

Take, for example, the company car. If the company owns the car and you use it for business purposes, the company is entitled to deduct operating and depreciation expenses as a valid business expense. If, however, you also use the car for pleasure, this value is calculated and added to your taxable income as a benefit received. On the other hand, if you own the vehicle and use it in the course of employment with a company, you would be entitled to deduct the business portion of operating expenses and depreciation from your personal income. Usually you would receive a separate allowance for the use of your car while on the job. You would be surprised how many employees operate on this basis and actually profit from the use of their cars (e.g., traveling sales representatives).

The important thing to remember is that both the company and the individual are entitled to deduct legitimate expenses incurred in the use of such assets, and where you have a close corporation in which employees and shareholders are the same persons, it makes no difference whether the company or the individual receives the benefit of these write-offs. Actually, there may be a slight difference, depending on the individual situation, because of the variance in individual and corporate tax rates. This is usually not significant enough to justify a wholesale transfer of assets into the company.

There is, however, one particular advantage to a transfer of assets into the company at the time of incorporation. Each partner makes a commitment to the new venture by "selling" an equal amount of assets to the company. Such a transfer psychologically locks the partners into the company. (It also makes the accounting easier).

It is simplest for the company to own the asset and deduct depreciation and operating expenses. If an employee owns the asset and rents it to the company, both the employee and the company will have to keep records of expenses.

Washington incorporators should also keep in mind that although no Washington sales tax is payable on the transfer of assets from a proprietor to a newly formed corporation, federal taxes can be a problem.

Finally, unless property sold to the corporation is actually paid for in cash, the incorporator or incorporators selling the property to the company may run the risk of not being paid in full for the property if the corporation encounters financial difficulties, goes out of business, or becomes bankrupt. In such a case, the seller would actually take a loss. Therefore, an alternative to selling personal or real property to the corporation is that the incorporators lease such property to the corporation on a long-term basis at fair and reasonable rates. The rent paid by the corporation is a business expense and is tax deductible by the corporation.

All leases with the corporation must be authorized by a resolution of the Board of Directors and be recorded in the minutes of the corporation. It is important that such leases provide that in the event of the bankruptcy of the corporation or its ceasing to do business, the leased property shall be returned to the lessors. The purpose of this type of an arrangement is to protect the lessor and prevent creditors of the corporation from reaching the leased property.

Remember, it is very easy to put assets into a corporation but sometimes difficult to get them out.

2. Transferring assets to the company

Basically, when you sell your asset to your corporation, the corporation must give something back in return as a payment for the debt. Some people prefer to receive a debt obligation rather than shares in exchange for their asset because, when the corporation pays off its debts, the money is considered as the repayment of a loan.

If you receive shares, your assets are forever tied up in the corporation and you will receive no direct benefits unless the corporation is wound up and the assets are sold at a profit, which is highly unlikely. A common form of payment is the demand note, as shown in Sample #20. A note like this can be prepared on behalf of the corporation in favor of each person transferring assets into the corporation.

As you can see, John Doe is entitled to "demand" payment at any time. What is to stop Mr. Doe from demanding payment immediately? First, he is not likely to demand payment unless he knows there are sufficient funds in the corporation's bank account to pay him. Second, if he had to sue, it would be tantamount to suing himself since he is the part owner of the "entity." So you see, a demand note payable to a shareholder-director of an incorporated partnership is usually a relatively safe proposition. Usually an informal agreement between the working "partners" as to where and when the notes should be presented for payment is quite sufficient.

If the corporation pays interest on the note to Mr. Doe, he has to pay tax on it. Interest payments made to the holder of the note are taxable in his hands. The principal amount is not taxable as it is analogous to the repayment of a loan made to the company.

There is one major risk in transferring assets to a company. If the corporation goes bankrupt or has judgments registered against it, the assets may be subject to seizure by creditors, in which case the debt owed to you by the corporation would be relegated to general creditor status and you would have to share in the proceeds of the resale of the assets along with the other creditors.

If you elect to transfer assets to your corporation via promissory notes, you should file a resolution in your corporate files. Sample #21 shows an example of such a resolution. Of course, you would alter it if you were receiving shares instead of a promissory note. Afterwards, you would contact the Department of Motor Vehicles, Motor-Vehicle Registration Division, Highways-Licenses Building, Olympia, Washington 98504, to change the registration of the motor vehicle involved in the transfer.

Whatever the method of transferring assets you use, be sure all transactions are accurately and fully documented.

3. Companies under section 351 of the code

When a corporation is formed, neither the transferor of the property (you) nor the recipient (your corporation) may recognize or claim a loss or gain if —

(a) the property is transferred to the corporation in exchange for shares only, and

(b) if you, the transferor, have control of the corporation immediately after the transfer takes place.

This situation arises because of the effect of section 351 of the Internal Revenue Code. This section allows you to transfer whatever assets you want to your own corporation free of federal tax so long as you meet the criteria listed above.

To fall within the section properly, you must assign all substantial rights in the property to the corporation. This means that the corporation usually has the right to sell or otherwise dispose of the goods. Special tax problems can arise when

SAMPLE #20
DEMAND NOTE

$2,000 *June 30, 199-*

ON DEMAND after the above date the corporation promises to pay to the order of *John Doe* at *Anywhere, Washington, Two Thousand Dollars ($2,000)* with interest at the rate of *ten percent (10%)* per annum, as well after as before maturity, FOR VALUE RECEIVED.

J & J PERSONNEL INC.

Per: John Doe
President

Jack Doe
Secretary

SAMPLE #21
RESOLUTION FOR THE TRANSFER OF ASSETS

IT WAS RESOLVED that the corporation purchase a motor vehicle and other equipment from the shareholder-director John Doe namely: 1987 Chevrolet, Serial Number 1234567B89, and that the said purchases be secured by promissory notes.

IT WAS RESOLVED that the corporation execute the said promissory note in such manner as required to give full effect to the transaction described above.

trademarks, franchises, and trade names are transferred to a company, and these should be given careful attention.

In order to have "control" within the scope of section 351, you must own at least 80% of the total combined voting power of all classes of stock entitled to vote and at least 80% of the total number of shares of all other classes of stock. Therefore, immediately after you have transferred assets to the corporation in exchange for shares alone you must own 80% or more of the total combined voting power of all classes of stock carrying voting rights.

You should be aware that problems can arise when the corporation assumes your liabilities along with your assets. The assumption of liabilities by the corporation merely reduces the adjusted basis of the stock received by you in the exchange (i.e., the stock is valued less). Where the nature of the liability and other circumstances indicate that you made the transfer in order to avoid tax or for some reason that was not a bona fide (honest) business purpose, then the transaction will be viewed as one which gives rise to tax liability.

Where the liabilities encumbering the property or assumed by the corporation exceed the total (aggregate) adjusted basis of all the property transferred, the excess is to be considered as a gain enjoyed by the transferor. This can be an expensive trap for unwary self-incorporators.

Note: The transfer of stock in exchange for your services to the corporation and the transfer of assets in return for corporate notes (promissory notes) has to be handled with care in order to fall within the exemptions provided by section 351.

g. DO YOU NEED A BUY-SELL AGREEMENT?

A buy-sell agreement is simply an agreement among the shareholders of a corporation that, on the happening of a certain event (usually the death or resignation of one of the partners), one or more of the remaining shareholders agree to purchase the shares of the deceased or departed person.

The purpose of it is to enable the existing shareholders to retain control of the corporation. For example, the death of a shareholder in a "close corporation" or "incorporated partnership" creates a serious situation for both the estate of the deceased shareholder and the surviving shareholders of the corporation.

From the point of view of the estate of the deceased shareholder, the shares of the corporation held by the deceased shareholder may have no market, as outsiders will seldom buy such shares unless the business is an established one and they are able to purchase the majority interest in the corporation. The only persons who may be interested in buying the shares may be the surviving shareholders. But if the deceased had a minority interest in the corporation, the surviving shareholders will retain control anyway, so they have no real need to buy the shares and may therefore be able to force the estate to sell the shares at bargain prices.

From the point of view of the typical close corporation, it may be very important to prevent the sale of the shares by the estate to a stranger or to someone with whom the remaining shareholders do not get along, or to prevent the shares being held by the beneficiaries of the deceased shareholder.

The death of a shareholder in a close corporation with no prior agreement as to the disposition of the shares may also adversely affect the credit position of the corporation because of uncertainty about the future of the business.

The only effective solution to these problems is for all the shareholders of the corporation to enter into a "buy-sell agreement." Under this type of agreement, the estate of a deceased shareholder is obligated to sell and the surviving shareholders are obligated to purchase all of the shares of the deceased or his or her heirs-at-law at a specified price or at a price to be determined under the agreement. Buy-sell agreements have the advantage of relative simplicity except where there are more than two or three parties, when this type of agreement can become very complicated.

Buy-sell agreements present two major problems:

(a) The funding of the purchase of the shares

(b) The valuation of the shares of the deceased

Usually, the funds for the purchase of the shares come from business life insurance policies under which each shareholder insures the lives of his or her fellow shareholders, and names himself or herself as the beneficiary of each policy. The idea is that the surviving shareholders will use the insurance proceeds to purchase the shares of the deceased shareholder from the estate of the deceased shareholder.

There are, of course, different types of life insurance and the decision as to which type should be obtained by the parties, the amount of insurance, and other related matters should be made only after consultation with an experienced life insurance underwriter.

The other problem may be dealt with in a number of ways, as no single method of valuation is appropriate to all types of business operations or circumstances.

There are five general methods by which shares can be valued:

(a) By using the valuation imposed by the estate tax authorities

(b) By some form of mixed formula (book value, capitalization of earnings, etc., or a combination of two or more of these methods)

(c) By some form of appraisal or arbitration

(d) By a fixed dollar amount by agreement among the parties, with or without a provision for periodic revaluation, or

(e) By a combination of two or more of these methods

The form of buy-sell agreement provided in this book is a very simple one and is provided only as a sample of what might be included in one (see Sample #22). You should obtain competent legal advice if you wish to enter into a buy-sell agreement unless you are certain about what you are doing.

SAMPLE #22
BUY-SELL AGREEMENT

BETWEEN:

JOHN DOE, Contractor, of *111 A Street*
in the City of *Anywhere,* in the State of Washington;

OF THE FIRST PART

AND:

JACK DOE, Accountant, of *222 B Street*
in the City of *Anywhere,* in the State of Washington;

OF THE SECOND PART

(hereinafter collectively called the "shareholders")

WHEREAS:

The shareholders own all the issued and outstanding shares of *J & J Personnel Inc.* a company incorporated under the laws of the State of Washington, having its head office in the City of *Seattle,* and consider it to be advantageous to themselves and to their respective estates to enter into an agreement whereby upon the death of one of them and the survival of the other, the estate of the deceased will be obligated to sell and the survivor will be obligated to purchase the shares owned by the deceased in the corporation; and

The parties wish to assure themselves that when the need arises the survivor will have sufficient monies available to pay in cash, one-half the purchase price for the shares of the deceased;

NOW THEREFORE in consideration of the mutual undertakings of the parties, the parties agree each with the other as follows:

1. On the death of either of the shareholders, the survivor will purchase all of the shares owned by the deceased in the corporation and the heirs, executors, administrators, or other legal representatives of the deceased, as the case may be, will sell, convey, and transfer all of the said shares to the survivor on the terms and conditions herein.

2. The purchase price to be paid for the shares as set out in paragraph 1 will be the amount calculated as set out in paragraph 5 (herein called the "calculated value").

3. The survivor will pay the heirs, executors, administrators, or other legal representatives the purchase price as follows:

(a) One-half in cash not later than 60 days after the date appropriate releases are secured to enable the shares to be transferred free and clear of any charge, lien, or encumbrance and the proceeds of insurance set out below are received;

(b) the balance thereof in 12 equal installments, the first of which will be paid on the same day of the third month following the date of the first payment and the second and succeeding installments will be paid on the same day of every third month thereafter until such time as the purchase price has been fully paid.

4. The balance of the purchase price outstanding from time to time will bear interest at the rate per annum which is equivalent to 1% per annum in excess of the prime commercial lending rate for the time being charged by *Super Savings Bank of Washington* on loans made by it to prime commercial borrowing customers, such interest to be calculated and be paid at the time of payment of each installment as aforesaid.

SAMPLE #22 — Continued

5. For the purpose of paragraph 2 hereof, the shareholders will cause the duly appointed auditors of the corporation *Larry Ledger & Co.*, or such other person or persons as the shareholders may in writing agree upon from time to time, to provide the shareholders with a calculated value each year immediately after the completion of the audited financial statements of the corporation. The calculated value will be:

(Here set out the basis for the valuation of the shares. See comments in text on the valuation of shares. Keep in mind that the value may depend on which shareholder has died — particularly in a two- or three-person corporation.)

6. Only annual financial statements which have been approved by each of the shareholders may be used for computing the calculated value.

7. Each of the shareholders will immediately purchase, and thereafter maintain in good standing, effective life insurance on the life of the other in the amount of $(insert amount)*.

**8. If at any time the calculated value is greater than $*100,000*, each of the shareholders will immediately purchase and maintain such additional life insurance upon the life of the other as is necessary to provide net insurance proceeds equal to the amount that would be payable by the survivor as set out in paragraph 3(a).

9. If either shareholder fails to make any payment required to maintain the life insurance on the other as provided for in the agreement, the other shareholder may make such payment on his or her behalf, and this amount will be payable by the insured immediately to the shareholder making such payment.

10. The parties will cause all policies of insurance on the life of each of the shareholders as provided in paragraphs 7 or 8 to provide that all proceeds will be payable to the other, his or her heirs, executors, and administrators. If any of such life insurance is used, with the written consent of all of the shareholders, as security for any loans or other financial obligations, such policies will be appropriately endorsed as to priority with the proviso that, upon discharge of any such loans or other financial obligation, the whole of the proceeds of the insurance policies will be payable as aforesaid.

11. If at the time of the death of one of the shareholders, the net proceeds of the insurance payable to the survivor on the death of the deceased are, for any reason, less than the amount required to be paid under paragraph 3(a), the payment required to be made under this paragraph 3(a) will be the amount of the insurance proceeds actually received by the survivor, and the difference between one-half the purchase price and the insurance proceeds actually received will be added to the amount to be paid in installments under paragraph 3(b) and the amount of each installment will be increased proportionately.

12. If both of the shareholders should die within 60 days of each other, this agreement will not be operative and the proceeds of all insurance provided for here will be paid to the respective estates of the shareholders.

13. This agreement will terminate automatically if the company is dissolved, wound up, or makes an assignment in bankruptcy, or if a receiving order is made against it under the Bankruptcy Act, or if the company otherwise acknowledges its insolvency. If this agreement is so terminated, each shareholder may, so long as he or she gives notice in writing to the

*The amount of life insurance needed is calculated by projecting the calculated value of the shares forward to the next review period (say one year) and dividing the total by the proportionate shareholdings of each individual.

**This clause is to allow for an automatic increase should there be no systematic review of insurance coverage.

other exercising the rights of assignment within 90 days after the termination of this agreement, receive from the other a full assignment of all the other's rights upon payment to the other of an amount equal to the cash surrender value of the policies of such insurance (if any) and thereafter the insurance will belong solely to the insured.

14. Except by mutual consent of the shareholders, neither of the shareholders may mortgage, charge, hypothecate, or otherwise deal with any shares in the company owned by him or her now or hereafter during the continuance of this agreement.

15. If on the death of one of the shareholders his or her shares are subject to any mortgage, hypothec or lien, or any other charge, the survivor may pay the amount required to release the shares, and the heirs, executors, administrators, or other legal representatives of the deceased will reimburse the survivor for such amount on demand.

16. The survivor will not be responsible for the payment of any estate taxes, succession duties, inheritance taxes, or other taxes which may be imposed as a result of the death of the deceased upon the interest of the deceased in the company or upon the proceeds of any insurance policies on the life of the deceased which are subject to this agreement.

17. This agreement will become operative and binding on the shareholders upon delivery by each to the other of certified copies of life insurance policies as provided in clause 7.

18. This agreement will be binding upon and enure to the benefit of the parties hereto and their respective heirs, executors, administrators, and successors.

IN WITNESS WHEREOF the parties have hereunto set their hands and seals this *26th* day of *May, 199-*.

SIGNED, SEALED, AND DELIVERED by — John Doe

in the presence of: — I. M. Witness

123 Incorporation Road, Seattle, Washington

SIGNED, SEALED, AND DELIVERED by — Jack Doe

in the presence of: — J. C Ewe

123 Incorporation Road, Seattle, Washington

6
COMPLYING WITH GOVERNMENT REGULATIONS

In the last decade, governments at all levels have intervened in our private lives and in private businesses on a massive scale.

For the small business person, this has meant a lot of headaches. I'm sure each of us has a pet peeve or can relate a particularly gruesome experience with government red tape.

Each of us develops our own defense mechanisms against pestering bureaucrats, such as, "It's in the mail," (particularly useful when the post office is on strike), or "I didn't receive it," or "I'm not in charge of that area" (classic reversal of the passing-the-buck mumble which government officials use), or "The person in charge of that is away on vacation."

If you don't mind the constant harassment, I suppose this practice can be carried on indefinitely. There is no doubt, however, that the entire exercise becomes counterproductive after a while.

My experience is that the best method is to explain to these officials that you are a small business person starting out and cannot afford the staff or time to comply with their requests. Frequently, in these situations, they will offer to send someone over to help you complete the form.

This is a great help because then all you have to do is answer questions, which is a lot easier than trying to interpret what they want on a form.

In any event, there are certain government licenses and regulations which will affect you and your business. Listed below is a summary of the things you need to know to keep your business and yourself in good standing with "Big Brother."

Books and records by your company will be audited from time to time. So, for this reason alone, you should establish an orderly records and accounts system which will be readily accessible from the beginning.

To do this you will need the help of a good accountant.

The best way to find someone is to ask your successful business friends, people you admire in a business sense, to supply you with names. Then talk to at least three of them before making a choice.

If you want to learn about accounting before you talk to an accountant so you can ask some intelligent questions, refer to *Basic Accounting for the Small Business*, another title in the Self-Counsel Series, for a simplified explanation of the accounting process.

a. YOU AND YOUR BOOKS

Aside from the pressure of government audits, the first motto of a small business corporation should in any case be, "Keep your books in order." Bookkeeping is an integral part of your business which records, summarizes, and analyzes your financial activity.

1. Reasons for good bookkeeping practices

You do not need books "just because the IRS tells you to keep books." You need a well-kept set of books because accurate, up-to-date information helps you make the best business decision possible. You cannot keep all aspects of your business inside your head. The total financial picture should be there for you to look at, especially where personal and corporate finances can mingle and become confused.

If you are involved in a retail business, or even providing services, you have to know how much your fixed costs, such as rent, utilities, taxes, supplies, and insurance, are costing you every day you open for business. Then you know what to charge, as you have a more complete idea of what it is costing you to sell.

As you know from reading chapter 5, you must open a bank account in your corporate name.

Some small business advisers suggest that it is easier to keep track of your business money by —

(a) paying all bills by check (or as many as possible),

(b) depositing all business income in the corporate account, and

(c) withdrawing all personal use money first, as a withdrawal or a personal draw, and then using the money to pay for personal items. In other words, never make use of the corporate money directly to pay for a personal item. Months later you won't remember what or who it was for. Furthermore, it will complicate your income tax calculation.

It is often a good idea to have an accountant, or competent bookkeeper, come in and train either an employee or yourself in how to properly keep usable business records.

2. Financial statements

No matter what legal form an organization may take, the preparation of meaningful financial statements is vital to any enterprise. This is because various people will have an interest in the financial affairs of the organization, namely owners, managers, creditors, the Internal Revenue Service, the state of Washington, and prospective buyers.

To illustrate, let us assume that you are a bank manager and that J & J Personnel Inc., a medium-sized corporation in the employment agency business, approaches you for a $10,000 loan. The principals explain that the funds are necessary for office expansion. As a prospective creditor you would be interested in two things: the ability of J & J Personnel Inc. to pay the regular installments of principal and interest on the loan and the amount you, the bank, would recover if the corporation could not meet its obligations.

To satisfy your curiosity in this regard, you would have to examine the financial statements of the corporation. The annual income would be shown on the profit and loss statement. This figure, if compared with the income from prior periods, would indicate to you the rate of economic growth of the enterprise.

In addition you would be able to determine whether or not enough total revenue is generated to repay the proposed loan. The balance sheet of the corporation would indicate any other long-term debt for which the corporation is liable. Furthermore, you would be able to determine which assets (inventories, accounts receivable, etc.) are available as security for the proposed loan.

The corporation's ability to pay its current obligations is another important indicator of the economic health of the enterprise. This ability to pay present debts when due can also be determined from the balance sheet. This indicator is expressed as a ratio (called the "current ratio") and is calculated by dividing the total current assets by the total current liabilities. This is illustrated in the very simple example in Sample #23.

Current assets exceed current liabilities in the ratio of 2:1. In other words, the working capital position of the corporation in this case is healthy.

In summary, you would obtain much of the information so vital to your decision regarding the loan by looking at the financial statements of J & J Personnel Inc.

The preceding illustration showed how financial statements can be useful to potential creditors. Furthermore, it is important to realize that financial statements are useful to anyone who has an interest (monetary or otherwise) in an enterprise. Just as certain medical implements are the tools by which a doctor can get some indication of physical health, so financial statements are the tools by which interested parties can measure the economic health of an organization.

Below is a breakdown, in point form, of the three major financial statements: the balance sheet, the profit and loss statement, and the earned surplus statement. They are discussed here to enable you to get some idea of the function and contents of financial statements.

(a) The balance sheet

The balance sheet is a position statement, not an historical record, and shows what is owned and owed at a given date.

There are three sections to a balance sheet: assets, liabilities, and owners' equity.

(i) Assets

Current assets are those assets which will be used up within one year of the current balance sheet date. Normal valuation of such assets is at original cost or market value, whichever is the lower.

Fixed assets are those assets which will provide benefits to the organization over a longer period than one year from the current balance sheet date. Valuation is generally at

SAMPLE #23
BALANCE SHEET (Partial)

J&J PERSONNEL INC.
MARCH 31, 199-

CURRENT ASSETS		CURRENT LIABILITIES	
Cash	$20,000	Trade payables	$100,000
Accounts receivable	290,000	Wages payable	10,000
Inventories	90,000	Current portion of long-term debt	90,000
TOTAL	**$400,000**	**TOTAL**	**$200,000**

original cost less accumulated depreciation. The amount of depreciation is based on the length of the useful life of the asset and the original cost of the asset.

To illustrate:

Building: original cost $20,000

Useful life: 10 years

Portion of asset cost which expires in each period:

$$\frac{\$20,000}{10} = 2,000$$

This type of depreciation is normally calculated on a reducing balance basis, but for illustrative purposes I have used the straight-line method. The sum of $2,000 is charged to the profit and loss statement in each period and is accumulated on the balance sheet as a reduction of the original cost of the asset. Thus, five years after the building was purchased, the balance sheet would show:

Building at cost	$20,000
Less accumulated depreciation (5 x $2,000)	10,000
Book value of building	$10,000

Because the asset may be sold for more than the original cost, the book value does not necessarily indicate the amount the equity-holders should receive for their ownership of the building. (**Note:** The "equity-holders" of the corporation are the shareholders.)

(ii) Liabilities and owner's equity

The nature of these items becomes evident in the illustration of a typical balance sheet (see Sample #24).

(b) Profit and loss statement

This statement indicates the profit or loss by subtracting the total expenses of a period from the total revenue for that period. There are two ways of determining when revenue is earned and when expenses are incurred:

(i) Cash basis

No revenue is recognized until cash is received. No expenses are recognized until cash is paid out.

(ii) Accrual basis

Revenue is recognized as soon as it is earned. Expenses are recognized as soon as they are incurred. The date cash is received or paid out is irrelevant.

(c) Earned surplus statement

This statement shows what happens to net profit. The last figure on a balance sheet represents earned surplus. This is the part of previous earnings retained by the corporation after providing for reserves and paying all operating expenses, accrued interest (on long-term loans), income taxes, and dividends.

The earned surplus belongs to the shareholder, but it is retained in the operation as a cushion to absorb possible losses, to protect the corporation from any other unforeseen occurrences, and as part of the capital of the operation.

b. MASTER BUSINESS APPLICATION

The sections that follow (sections **c.** to **f.**) explain the government regulations that apply to various businesses. Many of these regulations require you to obtain various registrations and licenses.

The state of Washington has now streamlined the first steps of organizing your paperwork by introducing a simplified "one-stop" Master Business Application. (See Sample #25.) You can use this application to obtain your registration for taxes, industrial insurance, and unemployment insurance, as well as many of the licenses you may need. The application form comes complete with detailed instructions, a list of fees, a description of requirements for each registration and license, a directory of offices where you can complete this "one-stop" application, and a federal employer identification application to allow you to establish a tax account for employees, corporations, and partnerships with the federal government.

You can obtain a Master Business Application form free from the Department of Revenue or from various state agencies.

c. YOU AND YOUR EMPLOYEES

Before you hire an employee, you should be aware that each employee will just about double your paperwork.

All employers must keep separate payroll records for each employee; withhold federal income tax, social security taxes, state income, and possibly state disability taxes; calculate quarterly and year-end payroll tax returns, the employer's portion of social security taxes and unemployment taxes; purchase workers' compensation insurance; and prepare year-end earnings statements for each employee.

Some have estimated that the paperwork involved and the necessary payments cost an additional 30% of the payroll. Therefore, if you pay an employee $3.00 per hour it is really costing you approximately $3.90 per hour by the time you pay for all the accompanying services.

In addition, there is no leeway or gray area given by the federal government or state governments in the area of payroll taxes. Your business could be locked up and the bank account impounded if you are even a few weeks late with your payroll tax returns.

Therefore, you should think it over carefully before deciding to hire a large number of employees. If you can hire what the IRS considers independent contractors, you might save yourself a lot of trouble.

An independent contractor is someone who is in business for himself or herself and differs from an employee in that the services he or she offers are to the public at large (and not limited to a single employer). Independent contractors have control over the method and results of the services they provide, and they determine when and how it shall be done. For example, you could hire a part-time person to come in and clean the office, and provide him or her with the necessary mops, brooms, and wash pails. On the other hand, you could avoid a lot of paperwork and payroll taxes by hiring a cleaning company to come in with its own equipment and clean the offices according to your instructions.

A doctor or dentist might hire an office services company to look after the filing, reservations, and supplies, rather than hiring an employee to do the same thing. I must stress that it is very important that you carefully consider the legal status of all those who do work for you. Even if you do not call a person an employee, he or she is an employee if IRS considers him or her to be one.

You will find the IRS pamphlet *Circular E — Employers' Tax Guide* (Publication #15) of great assistance if you are even considering becoming an employer. It is wise to get your orientation and identification process underway with the IRS and state agencies even before you actually hire anyone, because of the initial amount of paperwork.

You should note that if you do decide to hire an independent contractor, the only form you are responsible for is Form 1099 — Misc., which must be filed for every outside contractor to whom you pay more than $600 during the year.

1. Workers' compensation

Workers' compensation insurance provides the corporation with protection against liability for injuries incurred by employees. It also provides for payment of medical and hospital services and compensation for the employees during the time they are unable to work. Briefly stated, workers' compensation insurance covers all employees for injuries received in the course and scope of their employment, regardless of fault.

SAMPLE #24
BALANCE SHEET OF AN UNINCORPORATED BUSINESS

XYZ GROCERY
(Not Incorporated)
June 20, 199-

ASSETS

Current Assets			
Cash on hand and in bank		720.12	
Accounts receivable less allowance for doubtful accounts		657.72	
Merchandise inventory valued at the lower of original cost or market		3,212.63	
Prepaid expenses		157.55	
Total current assets			$4,748.02
Fixed Assets — At Cost			
Land		2,320.00	
Building	$5,767.16		
Less: accumulated depreciation	1,727.92	4,039.24	
Store fixtures	3,726.12		
Less: accumulated depreciation	982.36	2,743.76	
Delivery Truck	2,760.20		
Less: accumulated depreciation:	513.60	2,246.60	11,349.60
			16,097.62

LIABILITIES & PARTNERS' EQUITY

Current Liabilities			
Trade accounts payable		$2,772.18	
Accrued wages		75.20	
Employees' income tax payable		60.16	
Accrued real estate taxes		220.00	
Total current liabilities			3,127.54
Earned Surplus and Partner's Equity*			
Jones' share	$6,484.84		
Smith's share	$6,484.84		
			12,969.68
			$16,097.22

*If incorporated this would read as follows:

CAPITAL STOCK
Common stock, no par value — 100 shares.
Issued and fully paid for:
Jones — 50 shares at $1.00 = $50.00
Smith — 50 shares at $1.00 = $50.00
Retained earnings $12,969.68

If the corporation does not carry workers' compensation insurance and has made no other provisions for self-insurance, the corporation may become liable for penalties.

Sole proprietors and partners and corporate officers are exempt from mandatory coverage, although they may be included voluntarily if the Department of Labor and Industries approves. Certain casual employees who are not connected with the trade, profession, or business of the employer are also exempt from mandatory coverage. Following is a list of all industrial insurance offices for the state of Washington. Contact the one nearest you if you need help in completing the necessary registration forms.

Form LI 206 58 must be filed in order to open an industrial insurance account.

Department of Labor and Industries Local Service Locations

The U.S. Postal Service requests that mail be addressed to P.O. Box numbers, where available.

Aberdeen, 415 Wishkah, Suite 1B,
P.O. Box 66, 98520-0013
(360) 533-9300

Bellevue, 616 120th Ave. N.E., Suite C201,
98005-3037
(360) 453-6589

Bellingham, 2500 Elm St., Suite F,
98225-2732
(360) 676-2083

Bremerton, 4841 Auto Center Way,
Suite 201, 98312-4379
(360) 478-4921

Colville, 298 S. Main St., Suite 203,
99114-2416
(509) 684-7417

Ephrata, 21 C St. S.W., 98823-1895
(509) 754-4608

Everett, 8625 Evergreen Way, Suite 250,
98208-2620
(360) 290-1300

Kelso, 711 Vine St., 98626-2621
(360) 577-2200

Kennewick, 500 N. Morain St., Suite 1110A,
99336-2607
(509) 735-0100

Mount Vernon, 1220 Memorial Highway,
98273-3262
(360) 428-1350

Okanogan, 1234 2nd Ave. S., P.O. Box 632,
98840-0632
(509) 826-7345

Olympia, P.O. Box 44815, 98504-4815
(360) 956-5799

Port Angeles, 1026 E. First St., Suite 1,
98362-4020
(360) 457-2572

Seattle, 300 W. Harrison St., 98119-4081
(206) 281-5400

Spokane, 901 N. Monroe St., Suite 100,
99201-2111
(509) 324-2600

Tacoma, 1305 Tacoma Ave. S., Suite 305,
98402-1988
(206) 596-3800

Vancouver, 10401 N.E. Fourth Plain Road,
Suite 201, 98662-6302
(360) 696-6311
Portland, OR (503) 285-8747

Walla Walla, 1815 Portland Ave., Suite 2,
99362-2246
(509) 527-4437

Wenatchee, 123 Ohme Gardens Road,
Suite 203, 98801-9634
(509) 663-9713

Yakima, 1716 S. 16th Ave., 98902-5789
(509) 454-3700

2. Employment security

A corporation becomes subject to unemployment laws when it engages employees. However, since October 1, 1983, services performed by corporate officers as defined in the act are not considered services in employment. Thus, it is no longer necessary to carry unemployment coverage for corporate officers.

A corporation may, however, voluntarily elect to cover all of its corporate officers under RCW 50.24.160. If the corporation decides not to carry unemployment coverage for its corporate officers, it must notify its officers that they are ineligible for unemployment benefits.

Every employer of one or more people (except the above noted exemption for corporate officers) must file a Form EMS 5200 with the Employment Security Department. If a corporation elects voluntary coverage of its officers, it must file a Voluntary Election of Coverage form.

The nature of the license forms, the employee registration forms, and the industrial account forms is similar in that all require you to identify the nature of the business the corporation is going to engage in and to name the corporate officers and give their addresses. Scales and charts are provided with the forms to help you figure out what your premiums will be.

d. WASHINGTON STATE TAX CONSIDERATIONS

1. Tax registration

The Master Business License Application (as shown in Sample #25), begins the registration process with the Washington State Department of Revenue. Any person engaging in any type of business activity in Washington must register with the Department of Revenue. This application relates to business activity subject to business and occupation tax, retail sales tax, etc.

2. Real estate excise tax

The commissioners of any county in the state of Washington are authorized to levy an excise tax upon the sales of real estate. The proceeds of this tax go to the public schools.

The Washington Supreme Court has not ruled on the question of whether the transfer of real estate to a closely held corporation in exchange for its stock is a "sale" subject to the excise tax. The Attorney General has ruled that the transfer of real estate to a corporation by a transferor-shareholder in exchange for a capital stock of the corporation is a sale within the definition of RCW 82.45.010; the rationale being that a valuable consideration is received, namely, the certificates of capital stock. However, no tax is imposed on a transfer of property to a corporation that is wholly owned by the transferor, his or her spouse, or his or her children, unless either the corporation or the shareholders voluntarily retransfer the property or the stock within five years of the exchange, in which case, the excise tax becomes due on the value of the original transfer. If a resale is expected, you may consider leasing the property to the corporation as an alternative to transferring it outright.

3. Business and occupation tax

A tax is levied upon every person or corporation engaging in business activities. This tax varies depending upon the nature of the business, the gross proceeds from sales, or the gross income of the business, as the case may be. Transactions between a sole shareholder and his or her wholly owned corporation may be subject to the business and occupation tax.

Similarly, transactions between a parent and subsidiary corporation, including service fees such as accounting or management fees, are taxable.

4. Sales tax

All retail businesses in Washington become sales tax collectors for the state. Your collections will have to be remitted every quarter. You will remit the greatest proportion of the sales tax to the state and another, much smaller, percentage goes to the local government.

e. FEDERAL TAX CONSIDERATIONS

1. Employer identification number

Every new corporation must apply for a federal identification number on IRS Form SS-4 (Sample #26). Forms are available at any Internal Revenue Service or Social Security Administration office.

Internal Revenue also puts out a *Mr. Businessman's Kit*, which should be of great assistance to new businesses as it contains forms for federal taxes and explanations of how they are to be remitted.

Every corporation with employees must withhold income taxes and social security payments from the wages paid to employees. The amount to be withheld depends on marital status, number of dependents, and rate of pay. The amount of income taxes and social security payments to be withheld from employees' wages can be determined by using the IRS *Employer's Guide*.

2. Register for social security

Every employee must obtain a social security number by appearing personally at a Social Security Administration office and applying for a number.

When starting a new job, every employee must complete an IRS Form W-4, commonly known as the Employee's Withholding Allowance Certificate (see Sample #27). This certificate indicates the employee's marital status and number of dependents. It is used for determining the amount of federal taxes to be withheld from the employee's wages.

If an incorporator, director, officer, or shareholder is employed by a corporation and is paid for services performed, he or she is an employee and must have a social security number. All deductions must be withheld as in the case of any other employee.

The rate of the social security tax to be withheld from each employee's wages is 6.2%. An additional 1.45% must be withheld for medicare. The employer is required to contribute the same amount as is withheld.

At the end of each year the employer must compute the total compensation paid during the year to each employee, showing the total income tax withheld and the total social security deductions. These figures must be reported on IRS Form W-2 (Sample #28). The employer must deliver the original and a copy of Form W-2 to each employee. As well, the employer must send a copy of the W-2 form, along with a W-3 Transmittal Form (see Sample #29) to the IRS.

Keep in mind that all federal employee taxes are computed on a calendar year regardless of the corporation's fiscal year.

3. Federal unemployment tax

Every corporation is subject to the federal unemployment tax if it has one or more employees during each 20 calendar weeks in a calendar year or during the preceding year, or pays $1,500 or more during any calendar quarter in the current or preceding calendar year. The employer-corporation must pay to the IRS, 6.2% of wages paid to employees on the first $7,000 of wages paid during the calendar year.

The corporation is permitted to take a credit against its federal unemployment tax for contributions paid into the state unemployment fund of no more than 5.4% of the taxable wages.

The federal unemployment tax is imposed only upon employers and must not be deducted from the wages of employees. The employer must use IRS Form 940 in reporting the unemployment taxes.

When the taxes are deposited in an authorized commercial bank or federal reserve bank, the employer must use a federal tax deposit coupon. Form 940 is computed only once a year at the end of the calendar year.

The IRS furnishes guide pamphlets, forms, and charts of income and social

SAMPLE #25
MASTER BUSINESS APPLICATION

WASHINGTON STATE UBI UNIFIED BUSINESS IDENTIFIER

MASTER LICENSE SERVICE
DEPARTMENT OF LICENSING
P.O. BOX 9034
OLYMPIA, WA 98507-9034
Telephone: (360) 753-4401

UBI NUMBER
OWNER NAME (Please print clearly)

FOR VALIDATION – OFFICE USE ONLY

01P-400-731-0003

MASTER APPLICATION

Please type or print clearly in dark ink.

Take your completed application and fees to any location shown on the enclosed listing of offices, or MAIL DIRECTLY to the Master License Service.

A PAYMENT SUMMARY (Use the enclosed *Registration and License Description Sheet* for the information needed to complete this list.)

LIST REGISTRATIONS AND LICENSES BELOW		FEE
Tax Registration		$ No fee
Unemployment Insurance		$ No fee
Trade Name Registration		$ 5.00
		$
		$
		$
		$
Enclose check for **total** amount due, including application fee which MUST be submitted with this form. *Make check payable to the WASHINGTON STATE TREASURER.*	APPLICATION FEE	$ 15.00
	TOTAL AMOUNT DUE	$ 20.00

B PURPOSE OF APPLICATION (You may check more than one box, see the instructions on page 2.)

☒ Open/Reopen Business ☒ Register Trade Name ☐ Change Ownership ☐ Merger ☐ Hire Employees ☐ Hire Domestic Employees
☐ Add License/Registration ☐ Change Trade Name ☐ Open New Location ☐ Obtain Minor Work Permit ☐ Obtain License for Individual

C BUSINESS OWNERSHIP or INDIVIDUAL TO BE LICENSED (Complete appropriate section for business ownership type or provide information about individual to be licensed; see instructions on page 2.)

Check all that apply (see instructions): ☐ SOLE PROPRIETOR ☐ INDIVIDUAL TO BE LICENSED	Owner's Name *(Last, First, Middle)*	Birthdate	Social Security Number
	Home Address *(Street or Route, P.O. Box, City, State, Zip)*		Home Telephone Number ( )
	Spouse *(Last, First, Middle)* — Is the name of the spouse to appear on this license? ☐ YES ☐ NO	Social Security Number	COMPLETE ONLY FOR LIQUOR OR LOTTERY LICENSE — Birthdate
PARTNERSHIP List Partners in Section D	Partnership Name *(If any)* ☐ Limited *(If limited write name exactly as registered with Secretary of State)*		Number of Partners
	Partnership Mailing Address *(Street or Route, P.O. Box, City, State, Zip)*		
CORPORATION List Corporate Officers in Section D	Corporation Name *(Exactly as registered with Secretary of State)* J & J Personnel Incorporated		Date of Incorporation 31 May 199-
	Number of Corporate Officers 2	Are any Corporate Officers in Washington also Directors and Shareholders? ☒ YES ☐ NO	State of Incorporation WA
LIMITED LIABILITY COMPANY List Managers or Members in Section D	Company Name *(Exactly as registered with Secretary of State)*		Date of Formation
	Number of Managers (if no managers, number of members)		State of Formation
OTHER List Principals in Section D	Name of the Organization	Type of Organization	Business Mailing Address *(Street or Route, P.O. Box, City, State, Zip)*

If you need assistance through the Telecommunications Device for the Deaf, call TDD (360) 586-2788. To request this document in an alternate format for the visually impaired, call (360) 753-4401.

BLS-700-028 MASTER BUSINESS APP. (R/4/95)OR Page 1 of 4

Printed on Recycled Paper

INSTRUCTIONS

SECTION A: Payment Summary
Use the *Registration and License Description Sheet* to help you determine the fees, registrations, and licenses you need for yourself and/or your business. List the appropriate registrations, licenses, and fees in Section A.

SECTION B: Purpose of the Application
You may check more than one box in Section B. Each selection listed in Section B is described below. You may not need to complete the entire application, depending upon the purpose of your application.
Note: If the purpose for filing your application does not fit within the categories listed in section B, briefly describe the purpose of your application in section A. Complete **ALL** sections of the application.

- **Open/Reopen Business:** Check this box if:
  - You are operating a business in Washington for the first time.
  - You are reopening your business.

  Complete **ALL** sections of the application.
- **Add License/Registration:** Check this box if you are currently conducting business in this state and wish to add a license or registration. Complete sections A, B, C, E1, and K; complete section D if there are changes from the last filing.
  - If you are adding licenses that require additional forms (see *Registration and License Description Sheet*), please call Master License Service at (360) 753-4401 for the forms, or for information about licensing requirements for your business.
- **Register Trade Name:** You are required to register a Trade Name if you are a sole proprietor, partnership, corporation, or limited liability company conducting business in Washington under a name other than the **full legal name** listed in Section C. Complete sections A, B, C, E1, and K; complete section D if there are changes from the last filing. You may register more than one trade name for this business location.
- **Change Trade Name:** Check this box if you wish to cancel an existing Trade Name and register another Trade Name. List the Trade Name you wish to register and the fee amount in Section A. On the line below, enter the Trade Name you wish to cancel. Write "CANCEL" after that name. Complete sections A, B, C, E1, and K; complete section D if there are changes from the last filing.
- **Change Ownership:** Check this box if you are purchasing an existing business or making an ownership change. (For example: your business was a sole proprietorship, but is changing to a partnership.) Complete **ALL** sections of the application.
- **Open New Location:** Check this box if you are opening a new location for an existing business. Complete **ALL** sections of the application.
- **Merger:** Check this box if two businesses have merged to form a single business entity. Complete **ALL** sections of the application.
- **Obtain License for Individual:** Check this box if you are applying for a license for an individual. Complete sections A, B, C (*Sole Proprietor or Individual to be Licensed* portion), and K.
- **Hire Employees:** Check this box if you own an existing business and wish to hire employees. **A Master Business Application must be filed before employees can be hired.** Complete sections A, B, C, E1, J1, J2, and K; complete section D if there are changes from the last filing.
- **Obtain Minor Work Permit:** If you already have coverage for employees and are adding minors, complete sections A, B, C, E1, J1, and K; complete section D if there are changes from the last filing.
- **Hire Domestic Employees:** See *Registration and License Description Sheet* for definition of a domestic employee. Complete sections A, B, C (*Sole Proprietor or Individual to be Licensed* portion), J1, J2, and K. You do NOT have to pay the $15 application fee.

SECTION C: Business Ownership or Individual to be Licensed
Note: You may apply for a license for an individual and for business registrations and licenses on the same application. Follow the instructions below to ensure that you properly complete the application for both the individual license and the business registrations and licenses.

Individual: If you are applying for a license for an individual, check the appropriate box and complete the *Sole Proprietor/Individual to be Licensed* section. If you are applying only for an individual license, you do not need to complete the spouse information; if you are also applying for business licenses and registrations as a sole proprietor, this information should be provided.

Business: Determine which type of business ownership describes your business and complete the appropriate section. You may find the following ownership definitions helpful.

- **Sole Proprietor:** A self-employed owner operating a business for profit; or a marital community between spouses, unless a legal partnership exists.
- **Partnership:** An agreement between two or more entities engaged in the same business enterprise. Profits and losses are shared. Each partner is an agent for the other(s) and liable for the debts of the firm. Can also be a marital community who has formed a legal partnership.
- **Limited Partnership:** A partnership composed of general and limited partners. General partners are responsible for business management and losses. Limited partners are responsible only to the extent of their investments. *
- **Corporation:** A business entity that has the same rights and privileges as an individual. **Foreign (out-of-state) corporations** are corporations that have incorporated outside Washington. *
- **Limited Liability Company:** A business entity that is a hybrid between a partnership and a corporation that combines the operational flexibility of a partnership with the limited liability protection associated with limited partnerships and corporations. *
- **Other:** Unincorporated nonprofit associations, trusts, municipalities, political subdivisions, and others that do not fit any of the previous specific categories listed.

SECTION J: Employment
If you are planning to hire employees with a first date of employment more than three months after you file this application, the Departments of Employment Security and Labor & Industries will not open an account for you at this time. You will need to file another application before you hire employees.

---

* **Limited partnerships, corporations (domestic and foreign) and limited liability companies must file additional documents with the Office of the Secretary of State.** The name of a limited partnership, corporation or limited liability company is not guaranteed for use when entered on this application, unless that name has first been registered with the Office of the Secretary of State.

BLS-700-028 MASTER BUSINESS APP. (R/4/95)OR Page 2 of 4

SAMPLE #25 — Continued

UBI #

D PARTNERS, CORPORATE OFFICERS OR LIMITED LIABILITY COMPANY MANAGERS (or members if no managers were elected.)

Name (Last, First, Middle)	Birthdate	Social Security Number	% Owned
Doe John Alexander	2 June 1940	123-45-6789	50%

Home Address (Street or Route, P.O. Box, City, State, Zip)	Home Telephone Number	Title
111 A Street, Seattle WA	(206) 776-6667	President

Spouse (Last, First, Middle)	Social Security Number	COMPLETE ONLY FOR LIQUOR OR LOTTERY LICENSE	Birthdate
Doe Lucy Jean	222-44-5555		

Name (Last, First, Middle)	Birthdate	Social Security Number	% Owned
Doe Jack Richard	7 Oct. 1945	987-65-4213	50%

Home Address (Street or Route, P.O. Box, City, State, Zip)	Home Telephone Number	Title
222 B Street, Seattle WA	(206) 444-5566	Sec/Treas

Spouse (Last, First, Middle)	Social Security Number	COMPLETE ONLY FOR LIQUOR OR LOTTERY LICENSE	Birthdate
Doe Mary Sue	555-66-7777		

Name (Last, First, Middle)	Birthdate	Social Security Number	% Owned

Home Address (Street or Route, P.O. Box, City, State, Zip)	Home Telephone Number	Title
	( )	

Spouse (Last, First, Middle)	Social Security Number	COMPLETE ONLY FOR LIQUOR OR LOTTERY LICENSE	Birthdate

(Attach additional sheets if necessary.)

E BUSINESS INFORMATION (Complete for actual location where business will be conducted.)

E1

Date business first will be (was) conducted, under this owner, at this WA location: Mo Day Yr	
Firm/Trade Name	J & J Personnel Incorporated
Business Mailing Address (Street or Route, P.O. Box, Suite #— Do not use building name)	123 Incorporator Road
City	Seattle
State	WA
Zip	99999
Business Telephone Number	(206) 456-7890
Business Location (Street or Route, City, State, Zip — Physical location only)	123 Incorporator Road, Seattle WA 99999
FAX Number	(206) 456-7891

E2

Is this location within city limits?	☒ YES ☐ NO
If yes, which city?	Seattle
County	King
Total number of business locations you have in Washington	1
Is this business	☐ Part Time ☒ Full Time
Estimated Gross Annual Income in Washington (determines reporting frequency)	$150,000
Your Federal Employer I.D. Number (FEIN)	

Describe *in detail* the principal products sold or services you provide in Washington. Indicate if sales are retail or wholesale, and if products are manufactured in Washington:

Personnel Agency

Name and Address of Personal or Business Reference (Street or Route, P.O. Box, City, State, Zip)	Telephone Number
Joe Reference, 77 Speedy Avenue, Seattle WA 99999	(206) 789-1234

Bank Name (where you do banking)	Bank Branch Name
Savings Bank of Seattle	Downtown

Is this business owned by, controlled by, or affiliated with any other business entity?	☐ YES ☒ NO
If YES, list other business entity:	
Is this a Nonprofit Organization established for educational, religious, or charitable purposes?	☐ YES ☒ NO

F ANY OTHER BUSINESS (Complete this section if you are now or have ever been a sole proprietor, business partner, or owner of a corporation.)

Owner Name or Firm Name	Last year in business

Firm Address (Street or Route, P.O. Box, City, State and Zip)	UBI/State Tax Registration Number

G PRIOR OWNER (Complete this section if this business had a prior owner.)

Did you buy, lease or acquire all or part of an existing business?	☐ YES ☐ NO
If yes, check one box	☐ ALL ☐ PART
Date bought / leased / acquired (Mo Day Yr)	
Prior Business Name	
Prior Owner's Telephone No.	( )
Is prior owner still in business?	☐ YES ☐ NO
Prior Owner's Name and Address	

BLS-700-028 MASTER BUSINESS APP. (R/4/95)OR Page 3 of 4

SAMPLE #25 — Continued

H FURNITURE/FIXTURES/EQUIPMENT (Complete if you purchased or leased furniture, fixtures or equipment for this business.)

Did you purchase any fixtures or equipment on which you have not paid sales or use tax?	☒ YES ☐ NO	If Yes, purchase price $ 10,000	Are you leasing furniture, fixtures or equipment for use in Washington?	☐ YES ☒ NO	If Yes, from whom?

I OUT OF STATE BUSINESS (Complete if your business is based outside of Washington.)

Are sales solicited on your behalf in Washington?	☐ YES ☐ NO	If Yes, by: ☐ Resident employees ☐ Non-resident employees ☐ Traveling representatives	☐ Local independent agents ☐ Other

Do you maintain stocks of merchandise, including consigned stock, in Washington?	☐ YES ☐ NO	Do you lease articles of personal property to others for use in Washington?	☐ YES ☐ NO	Do you perform services in Washington for customers, clients, or franchisees?	☐ YES ☐ NO

J EMPLOYMENT (Complete if you employ, or plan to employ, one or more persons in Washington; or if you want optional coverage.)

J1 Date of first employment or planned employment at this location (Mo Day Yr)	Number of persons you employ or plan to employ at this location *(Do not include owners)*	Of these, how many are or will be minors *(under age 18)*?	Are any of these minors under age 16? ☐ YES ☐ NO

List the specific duties performed by minors at this location

Are the minors working in an agricultural business? ☐ YES ☐ NO

J2 If you operate at more than one location, do you wish to report your locations together or separately? ☐ TOGETHER ☐ SEPARATELY

Do you wish Unemployment Insurance coverage for corporate officers? ☒ Yes — Completed Form 5203 is required. This form will be sent to you by Employment Security Department. ☐ No — Officers must be informed in writing by the corporation.

The following categories of employment ARE NOT INCLUDED under the mandatory coverage laws of Washington for Industrial Insurance (if you would like Industrial Insurance coverage for any of these categories, you must request optional coverage below):

Sole proprietor/partner or corporate officers who are directors and shareholders; domestic servants; gardening/maintenance/remodeling in or about the employers home; services in return for aid; minors under 18 years employed on a family farm; jockey-racing; entertainers; volunteer law enforcement; volunteer workers or student volunteers (K thru 12) (medical only); Indian tribal members; community service workers; cosmetologists, barbers, and manicurists who rent booths; newspaper carriers; insurance agents, brokers, and solicitors; other employment as defined in Title 51 of the Revised Code of Washington.

Indicate if you wish coverage for:
Sole proprietor, partner or corporate officers who are directors and shareholders .... ☐ YES ☐ NO
Optional coverage for excluded employment .... ☐ YES ☐ NO (If yes, write category from above list in employee activity section below.)

Coverage is effective as of the date this form is received, unless a later date is requested (indicate requested date in section below). A letter confirming coverage and providing information and instructions will be provided when the application is processed. Coverage will remain in effect until notification to cancel has been filed by the employer and received by the Department of Labor & Industries.

You must check the ONE box which best describes the major operation of your business:

(01) ☐ Construction — Wood Frame Bldg.	(05) ☐ Shipbuilding	(09) ☐ Mfg. — Food Products	(13) ☐ Retail / Wholesale Trade
(02) ☐ Construction — All Other	(06) ☐ Mining / Quarrying / Sand & Gravel	(10) ☐ Miscellaneous Mfg.	(14) ☐ Services or Operations or Maintenance
(03) ☐ Logging / Forestry	(07) ☐ Mfg. — Wood / Metal / Stone Products	(11) ☐ Machine Shops / Auto Repair	(15) ☐ Communications
(04) ☐ Temporary Help or Trucking	(08) ☐ Mfg. — Chemicals	(12) ☐ Agricultural / Farming	(16) ☐ Clerical / Professional Occup.

DESCRIBE IN DETAIL THE ACTIVITIES OF YOUR EMPLOYEES AND/OR INDICATE THE CATEGORY OF OPTIONAL COVERAGE REQUESTED AND EFFECTIVE DATE	3 MONTH ESTIMATE Number of Employees	Workers hours (include minors)

K SIGNATURE (of sole proprietor or spouse, partner(s), corporate officer(s), or limited liability manager(s) or member(s).)

I (we), the undersigned, declare under the penalties of perjury and/or the revocation of any license granted, that I (we) am (are) the applicant(s) or authorized representative(s) of the firm making this application and that the answers contained, including any accompanying information have been examined by me (us) and that the matters and things set forth are true, correct and complete.

Signature(s) required (If a corp., corporate officer must sign; if a limited liability co., manager must sign)	Title	Date
X John Doe	President	May 10, 199-
X Jack Doe	Secretary-Treasurer	May 10, 199-
X		

Application prepared by *(please print)*	Title	Telephone number	Date
John Doe	President	206-456-7890	May 10, 199-

Agency representative assisting with application *(Please print)*	☐ Mail ☐ Counter	Agency Office	Telephone number	Date

BLS-700-028 MASTER BUSINESS APP. (R/4/95)OR Page 4 of 4

SAMPLE #26
APPLICATION FOR EMPLOYER IDENTIFICATION NUMBER

Form **SS-4** (Rev. December 1993)
Department of the Treasury
Internal Revenue Service

Application for Employer Identification Number

(For use by employers, corporations, partnerships, trusts, estates, churches, government agencies, certain individuals, and others. See instructions.)

EIN

OMB No. 1545-0003
Expires 12-31-96

Please type or print clearly.

1 Name of applicant (Legal name) (See instructions.)
J & J Personnel Incorporated

2 Trade name of business, if different from name in line 1
J & J Personnel Inc.

3 Executor, trustee, "care of" name

4a Mailing address (street address) (room, apt., or suite no.)
123 Incorporator Road

5a Business address, if different from address in lines 4a and 4b

4b City, state, and ZIP code
Seattle, WA 99999

5b City, state, and ZIP code

6 County and state where principal business is located
King County, Washington

7 Name of principal officer, general partner, grantor, owner, or trustor—SSN required (See instructions.) ►
John A. Doe 123-45-6789

8a Type of entity (Check only one box.) (See instructions.)
☐ Sole Proprietor (SSN)
☐ REMIC
☐ Personal service corp.
☐ State/local government
☐ National guard
☐ Other nonprofit organization (specify) ______ (enter GEN if applicable) ______
☐ Other (specify) ►
☐ Estate (SSN of decedent)
☐ Plan administrator-SSN
☒ Other corporation (specify) Personnel Agency
☐ Federal government/military
☐ Church or church controlled organization
☐ Trust
☐ Partnership
☐ Farmers' cooperative

8b If a corporation, name the state or foreign country (if applicable) where incorporated ►
State: Washington
Foreign country:

9 Reason for applying (Check only one box.)
☒ Started new business (specify) ►
☐ Hired employees
☐ Created a pension plan (specify type) ►
☐ Banking purpose (specify) ►
☐ Changed type of organization (specify) ►
☐ Purchased going business
☐ Created a trust (specify) ►
☐ Other (specify) ►

10 Date business started or acquired (Mo., day, year) (See instructions.)
May 31, 199-

11 Enter closing month of accounting year. (See instructions.)
December

12 First date wages or annuities were paid or will be paid (Mo., day, year). **Note:** *If applicant is a withholding agent, enter date income will first be paid to nonresident alien. (Mo., day, year)* ► June 1, 199-

13 Enter highest number of employees expected in the next 12 months. **Note:** *If the applicant does not expect to have any employees during the period, enter "0."* ►

Nonagricultural	Agricultural	Household
3	0	0

14 Principal activity (See instructions.) ► Personnel Agency

15 Is the principal business activity manufacturing? ☐ **Yes** ☒ **No**
If "Yes," principal product and raw material used ►

16 To whom are most of the products or services sold? Please check the appropriate box.
☒ Business (wholesale)
☐ Public (retail)
☐ Other (specify) ►
☐ N/A

17a Has the applicant ever applied for an identification number for this or any other business? ☐ **Yes** ☒ **No**
Note: *If "Yes," please complete lines 17b and 17c.*

17b If you checked the "Yes" box in line 17a, give applicant's legal name and trade name, if different than name shown on prior application.
Legal name ►
Trade name ►

17c Enter approximate date, city, and state where the application was filed and the previous employer identification number if known.

Approximate date when filed (Mo., day, year)	City and state where filed	Previous EIN

Under penalties of perjury, I declare that I have examined this application, and to the best of my knowledge and belief, it is true, correct, and complete.

Business telephone number (include area code): (206) 456-7890

Name and title (Please type or print clearly.) ► President

Signature ► John Doe

Date ► May 10, 199-

Note: *Do not write below this line. For official use only.*

Please leave blank ►	Geo.	Ind.	Class	Size	Reason for applying

For Paperwork Reduction Act Notice, see attached instructions. Cat. No. 16055N Form **SS-4** (Rev. 12-93)

General Instructions

(Section references are to the Internal Revenue Code unless otherwise noted.)

Purpose

Use Form SS-4 to apply for an employer identification number (EIN). An EIN is a nine-digit number (for example, 12-3456789) assigned to sole proprietors, corporations, partnerships, estates, trusts, and other entities for filing and reporting purposes. The information you provide on this form will establish your filing and reporting requirements.

Who Must File

You must file this form if you have not obtained an EIN before and

- You pay wages to one or more employees.
- You are required to have an EIN to use on any return, statement, or other document, even if you are not an employer.
- You are a withholding agent required to withhold taxes on income, other than wages, paid to a nonresident alien (individual, corporation, partnership, etc.). A withholding agent may be an agent, broker, fiduciary, manager, tenant, or spouse, and is required to file **Form 1042,** Annual Withholding Tax Return for U.S. Source Income of Foreign Persons.
- You file **Schedule C,** Profit or Loss From Business, or **Schedule F,** Profit or Loss From Farming, of **Form 1040,** U.S. Individual Income Tax Return, and have a Keogh plan or are required to file excise, employment, or alcohol, tobacco, or firearms returns.

The following must use EINs even if they do not have any employees:

- Trusts, except the following:

1. Certain grantor-owned revocable trusts (see the Instructions for Form 1040).

2. Individual Retirement Arrangement (IRA) trusts, unless the trust has to file **Form 990-T,** Exempt Organization Business Income Tax Return (See the Instructions for Form 990-T.)

- Estates
- Partnerships
- REMICS (real estate mortgage investment conduits) (See the instructions for **Form 1066,** U.S. Real Estate Mortgage Investment Conduit Income Tax Return.)
- Corporations
- Nonprofit organizations (churches, clubs, etc.)
- Farmers' cooperatives
- Plan administrators (A plan administrator is the person or group of persons specified as the administrator by the instrument under which the plan is operated.)

Note: *Household employers are not required to file Form SS-4 to get an EIN. An EIN may be assigned to you without filing Form SS-4 if your only employees are household employees (domestic workers) in your private home. To have an EIN assigned to you, write "NONE" in the space for the EIN on* ***Form 942,*** *Employer's Quarterly Tax Return for Household Employees, when you file it.*

When To Apply for A New EIN

New Business.—If you become the new owner of an existing business, **DO NOT** use the EIN of the former owner. If you already have an EIN, use that number. If you do not have an EIN, apply for one on this form. If you become the "owner" of a corporation by acquiring its stock, use the corporation's EIN.

Changes in Organization or Ownership.—If you already have an EIN, you may need to get a new one if either the organization or ownership of your business changes. If you incorporate a sole proprietorship or form a partnership, you must get a new EIN. However, **DO NOT** apply for a new EIN if you change only the name of your business.

File Only One Form SS-4.—File only one Form SS-4, regardless of the number of businesses operated or trade names under which a business operates. However, each corporation in an affiliated group must file a separate application.

EIN Applied For, But Not Received.—If you do not have an EIN by the time a return is due, write "Applied for" and the date you applied in the space shown for the number. **DO NOT** show your social security number as an EIN on returns.

If you do not have an EIN by the time a tax deposit is due, send your payment to the Internal Revenue service center for your filing area. (See **Where To Apply** below.) Make your check or money order payable to Internal Revenue Service and show your name (as shown on Form SS-4), address, kind of tax, period covered, and date you applied for an EIN.

For more information about EINs, see **Pub. 583,** Taxpayers Starting a Business and **Pub. 1635,** EINs Made Easy.

How To Apply

You can apply for an EIN either by mail or by telephone. You can get an EIN immediately by calling the Tele-TIN phone number for the service center for your state, or you can send the completed Form SS-4 directly to the service center to receive your EIN in the mail.

Application by Tele-TIN.—Under the Tele-TIN program, you can receive your EIN over the telephone and use it immediately to file a return or make a payment. To receive an EIN by phone, complete Form SS-4, then call the Tele-TIN phone number listed for your state under **Where To Apply.** The person making the call must be authorized to sign the form (see **Signature block** on page 3).

An IRS representative will use the information from the Form SS-4 to establish your account and assign you an EIN. Write the number you are given on the upper right-hand corner of the form, sign and date it.

You should mail or FAX the signed SS-4 ***within 24 hours*** *to the Tele-TIN Unit at the service center address for your state.* The IRS representative will give you the FAX number. The FAX numbers are also listed in Pub. 1635.

Taxpayer representatives can receive their client's EIN by phone if they first send a facsimile (FAX) of a completed **Form 2848,** Power of Attorney and Declaration of Representative, or **Form 8821,** Tax Information Authorization, to the Tele-TIN unit. The Form 2848 or Form 8821 will be used solely to release the EIN to the representative authorized on the form.

Application by Mail.—Complete Form SS-4 at least 4 to 5 weeks before you will need an EIN. Sign and date the application and mail it to the service center address for your state. You will receive your EIN in the mail in approximately 4 weeks.

Where To Apply

The Tele-TIN phone numbers listed below will involve a long-distance charge to callers outside of the local calling area, and should be used only to apply for an EIN. THE NUMBERS MAY CHANGE WITHOUT NOTICE. Use 1-800-829-1040 to verify a number or to ask about an application by mail or other Federal tax matters.

If your principal business, office or agency, or legal residence in the case of an individual, is located in:	Call the Tele-TIN phone number shown or file with the Internal Revenue Service center at:
Florida, Georgia, South Carolina	Attn: Entity Control Atlanta, GA 39901 (404) 455-2360
New Jersey, New York City and counties of Nassau, Rockland, Suffolk, and Westchester	Attn: Entity Control Holtsville, NY 00501 (516) 447-4955
New York (all other counties), Connecticut, Maine, Massachusetts, New Hampshire, Rhode Island, Vermont	Attn: Entity Control Andover, MA 05501 (508) 474-9717
Illinois, Iowa, Minnesota, Missouri, Wisconsin	Attn: Entity Control Stop 57A 2306 E. Bannister Rd. Kansas City, MO 64131 (816) 926-5999
Delaware, District of Columbia, Maryland, Pennsylvania, Virginia	Attn: Entity Control Philadelphia, PA 19255 (215) 574-2400

SAMPLE #26 — Continued

Indiana, Kentucky, Michigan, Ohio, West Virginia	Attn: Entity Control Cincinnati, OH 45999 (606) 292-5467
Kansas, New Mexico, Oklahoma, Texas	Attn: Entity Control Austin, TX 73301 (512) 462-7843
Alaska, Arizona, California (counties of Alpine, Amador, Butte, Calaveras, Colusa, Contra Costa, Del Norte, El Dorado, Glenn, Humboldt, Lake, Lassen, Marin, Mendocino, Modoc, Napa, Nevada, Placer, Plumas, Sacramento, San Joaquin, Shasta, Sierra, Siskiyou, Solano, Sonoma, Sutter, Tehama, Trinity, Yolo, and Yuba), Colorado, Idaho, Montana, Nebraska, Nevada, North Dakota, Oregon, South Dakota, Utah, Washington, Wyoming	Attn: Entity Control Mail Stop 6271-T P.O. Box 9950 Ogden, UT 84409 (801) 620-7645
California (all other counties), Hawaii	Attn: Entity Control Fresno, CA 93888 (209) 452-4010
Alabama, Arkansas, Louisiana, Mississippi, North Carolina, Tennessee	Attn: Entity Control Memphis, TN 37501 (901) 365-5970

If you have no legal residence, principal place of business, or principal office or agency in any state, file your form with the Internal Revenue Service Center, Philadelphia, PA 19255 or call (215) 574-2400.

Specific Instructions

The instructions that follow are for those items that are not self-explanatory. Enter N/A (nonapplicable) on the lines that do not apply.

Line 1.—Enter the legal name of the entity applying for the EIN exactly as it appears on the social security card, charter, or other applicable legal document.

Individuals.—Enter the first name, middle initial, and last name.

Trusts.—Enter the name of the trust.

Estate of a decedent.—Enter the name of the estate.

Partnerships.—Enter the legal name of the partnership as it appears in the partnership agreement.

Corporations.—Enter the corporate name as set forth in the corporation charter or other legal document creating it.

Plan administrators.—Enter the name of the plan administrator. A plan administrator who already has an EIN should use that number.

Line 2.—Enter the trade name of the business if different from the legal name. The trade name is the "doing business as" name.

Note: *Use the full legal name on line 1 on all tax returns filed for the entity. However, if you enter a trade name on line 2 and choose to use the trade name instead of the legal name, enter the trade name on all returns you file. To prevent processing delays and errors,* ***always*** *use either the legal name only or the trade name only on all tax returns.*

Line 3.—Trusts enter the name of the trustee. Estates enter the name of the executor, administrator, or other fiduciary. If the entity applying has a designated person to receive tax information, enter that person's name as the "care of" person. Print or type the first name, middle initial, and last name.

Line 7.—Enter the first name, middle initial, last name, and social security number (SSN) of a principal officer if the business is a corporation; of a general partner if a partnership; and of a grantor owner, or trustor if a trust.

Line 8a.—Check the box that best describes the type of entity applying for the EIN. If not specifically mentioned, check the "other" box and enter the type of entity. Do not enter N/A.

Sole proprietor.—Check this box if you file Schedule C or F (Form 1040) and have a Keogh plan, or are required to file excise, employment, or alcohol, tobacco, or firearms returns. Enter your SSN (social security number) in the space provided.

Plan administrator.—If the plan administrator is an individual, enter the plan administrator's SSN in the space provided.

Withholding agent.—If you are a withholding agent required to file Form 1042, check the "other" box and enter "withholding agent."

REMICs.—Check this box if the entity has elected to be treated as a real estate mortgage investment conduit (REMIC). See the Instructions for Form 1066 for more information.

Personal service corporations.—Check this box if the entity is a personal service corporation. An entity is a personal service corporation for a tax year only if:

- The principal activity of the entity during the testing period (prior tax year) for the tax year is the performance of personal services substantially by employee-owners.
- The employee-owners own 10 percent of the fair market value of the outstanding stock in the entity on the last day of the testing period.

Personal services include performance of services in such fields as health, law, accounting, consulting, etc. For more information about personal service corporations, see the instructions to **Form 1120,** U.S. Corporation Income Tax Return, and **Pub. 542,** Tax Information on Corporations.

Other corporations.—This box is for any corporation other than a personal service corporation. If you check this box, enter the type of corporation (such as insurance company) in the space provided.

Other nonprofit organizations.—Check this box if the nonprofit organization is other than a church or church-controlled organization and specify the type of nonprofit organization (for example, an educational organization.)

If the organization also seeks tax-exempt status, you must file either **Package 1023** or **Package 1024,** Application for Recognition of Exemption. Get **Pub. 557,** Tax-Exempt Status for Your Organization, for more information.

Group exemption number (GEN).—If the organization is covered by a group exemption letter, enter the four-digit GEN. (Do not confuse the GEN with the nine-digit EIN.) If you do not know the GEN, contact the parent organization. Get Pub. 557 for more information about group exemption numbers.

Line 9.—Check only **one** box. Do not enter N/A.

Started new business.—Check this box if you are starting a new business that requires an EIN. If you check this box, enter the type of business being started. **DO NOT** apply if you already have an EIN and are only adding another place of business.

Changed type of organization.—Check this box if the business is changing its type of organization, for example, if the business was a sole proprietorship and has been incorporated or has become a partnership. If you check this box, specify in the space provided the type of change made, for example, "from sole proprietorship to partnership."

Purchased going business.—Check this box if you purchased an existing business. DO NOT use the former owner's EIN. Use your own EIN if you already have one.

Hired employees.—Check this box if the existing business is requesting an EIN because it has hired or is hiring employees and is therefore required to file employment tax returns. **DO NOT** apply if you already have an EIN and are only hiring employees. If you are hiring household employees, see **Note** under **Who Must File** on page 2.

Created a trust.—Check this box if you created a trust, and enter the type of trust created.

Note: *DO NOT file this form if you are the individual-grantor/owner of a revocable trust. You must use your SSN for the trust. See the instructions for Form 1040.*

Created a pension plan.—Check this box if you have created a pension plan and need this number for reporting purposes. Also, enter the type of plan created.

Banking purpose.—Check this box if you are requesting an EIN for banking purposes only and enter the banking purpose (for example, a bowling league for depositing dues, an investment club for dividend and interest reporting, etc.).

SAMPLE #26 — Continued

Other (specify).—Check this box if you are requesting an EIN for any reason other than those for which there are checkboxes, and enter the reason.

Line 10.—If you are starting a new business, enter the starting date of the business. If the business you acquired is already operating, enter the date you acquired the business. Trusts should enter the date the trust was legally created. Estates should enter the date of death of the decedent whose name appears on line 1 or the date when the estate was legally funded.

Line 11.—Enter the last month of your accounting year or tax year. An accounting or tax year is usually 12 consecutive months, either a calendar year or a fiscal year (including a period of 52 or 53 weeks). A calendar year is 12 consecutive months ending on December 31. A fiscal year is either 12 consecutive months ending on the last day of any month other than December or a 52-53 week year. For more information on accounting periods, see **Pub. 538,** Accounting Periods and Methods.

Individuals.—Your tax year generally will be a calendar year.

Partnerships.—Partnerships generally must adopt the tax year of either (1) the majority partners; (2) the principal partners; (3) the tax year that results in the least aggregate (total) deferral of income; or (4) some other tax year. (See the Instructions for **Form 1065,** U.S. Partnership Return of Income, for more information.)

REMICs.—Remics must have a calendar year as their tax year.

Personal service corporations.—A personal service corporation generally must adopt a calendar year unless:

- It can establish a business purpose for having a different tax year, or
- It elects under section 444 to have a tax year other than a calendar year.

Trusts.—Generally, a trust must adopt a calendar year except for the following:

- Tax-exempt trusts,
- Charitable trusts, and
- Grantor-owned trusts.

Line 12.—If the business has or will have employees, enter the date on which the business began or will begin to pay wages. If the business does not plan to have employees, enter N/A.

Withholding agent.—Enter the date you began or will begin to pay income to a nonresident alien. This also applies to individuals who are required to file Form 1042 to report alimony paid to a nonresident alien.

Line 14.—Generally, enter the exact type of business being operated (for example, advertising agency, farm, food or beverage establishment, labor union, real estate agency, steam laundry, rental of coin-operated vending machine, investment club, etc.). Also state if the business will involve the sale or distribution of alcoholic beverages.

Governmental.—Enter the type of organization (state, county, school district, or municipality, etc.).

Nonprofit organization (other than governmental).—Enter whether organized for religious, educational, or humane purposes, and the principal activity (for example, religious organization—hospital, charitable).

Mining and quarrying.—Specify the process and the principal product (for example, mining bituminous coal, contract drilling for oil, quarrying dimension stone, etc.).

Contract construction.—Specify whether general contracting or special trade contracting. Also, show the type of work normally performed (for example, general contractor for residential buildings, electrical subcontractor, etc.).

Food or beverage establishments.—Specify the type of establishment and state whether you employ workers who receive tips (for example, lounge—yes).

Trade.—Specify the type of sales and the principal line of goods sold (for example, wholesale dairy products, manufacturer's representative for mining machinery, retail hardware, etc.).

Manufacturing.—Specify the type of establishment operated (for example, sawmill, vegetable cannery, etc.).

Signature block.—The application must be signed by: (1) the individual, if the applicant is an individual, (2) the president, vice president, or other principal officer, if the applicant is a corporation, (3) a responsible and duly authorized member or officer having knowledge of its affairs, if the applicant is a partnership or other unincorporated organization, or (4) the fiduciary, if the applicant is a trust or estate.

Some Useful Publications

You may get the following publications for additional information on the subjects covered on this form. To get these and other free forms and publications, call 1-800-TAX-FORM (1-800-829-3676).

Pub. 1635, EINs Made Easy

Pub. 538, Accounting Periods and Methods

Pub. 541, Tax Information on Partnerships

Pub. 542, Tax Information on Corporations

Pub. 557, Tax-Exempt Status for Your Organization

Pub. 583, Taxpayers Starting A Business

Pub. 937, Employment Taxes and Information Returns

Package 1023, Application for Recognition of Exemption

Package 1024, Application for Recognition of Exemption Under Section 501(a) or for Determination Under Section 120

Paperwork Reduction Act Notice

We ask for the information on this form to carry out the Internal Revenue laws of the United States. You are required to give us the information. We need it to ensure that you are complying with these laws and to allow us to figure and collect the right amount of tax.

The time needed to complete and file this form will vary depending on individual circumstances. The estimated average time is:

Recordkeeping . . . . . . 7 min.

Learning about the law or the form . . . . . . 18 min.

Preparing the form . . . . . 44 min.

Copying, assembling, and sending the form to the IRS . 20 min.

If you have comments concerning the accuracy of these time estimates or suggestions for making this form more simple, we would be happy to hear from you. You can write to both the **Internal Revenue Service,** Attention: Reports Clearance Officer, PC:FP, Washington, DC 20224; and the **Office of Management and Budget,** Paperwork Reduction Project (1545-0003), Washington, DC 20503. **DO NOT** send this form to either of these offices. Instead, see **Where To Apply** on page 2.

Printed on recycled paper

*U.S. Government Printing Office: 1994 — 387-095/00295

SAMPLE #27
EMPLOYEE'S WITHHOLDING ALLOWANCE CERTIFICATE
(Form W-4)

Form **W-4** (Rev. January 1984)

Department of the Treasury—Internal Revenue Service

Employee's Withholding Allowance Certificate

OMB No. 1545-0010

1 Type or print your full name Ella Employee	2 Your social security number 000-00-0000
Home address (number and street or rural route) 910 Work Street, City or town, State, and ZIP code Anywhere, WA 99999	3 Marital Status: [x] Single [ ] Married [ ] Married, but withhold at higher Single rate **Note:** If married, but legally separated, or spouse is a nonresident alien, check the Single box.

4 Total number of allowances you are claiming (from line F of the worksheet on page 2) 2

5 Additional amount, if any, you want deducted from each pay . . . . $ 0

6 I claim exemption from withholding because (see instructions and check boxes below that apply):

a [ ] Last year I did not owe any Federal income tax and had a right to a full refund of **ALL** income tax withheld, **AND**

b [ ] This year I do not expect to owe any Federal income tax and expect to have a right to a full refund of **ALL** income tax withheld. If both a and b apply, enter the year effective and "EXEMPT" here . . . ▶ Year

c If you entered "EXEMPT" on line 6b, are you a full-time student? . . . . [ ] **Yes** [ ] **No**

Under penalties of perjury, I certify that I am entitled to the number of withholding allowances claimed on this certificate, or if claiming exemption from withholding, that I am entitled to claim the exempt status.

Employee's signature ▶ Date ▶ , 19

7 Employer's name and address **(Employer: Complete 7, 8, and 9 only if sending to IRS)**	8 Office code	9 Employer identification number
J & J Personnel Inc., 123 Incorporator Rd. Anywhere, WA 99999	XB	0101011

Detach along this line. Give the top part of this form to employer; keep the lower part for your records.

SAMPLE #28
WAGE AND TAX STATEMENT
(Form W-2)

a Control number 22222	Void [ ]	**For Official Use Only** ▶ OMB No. 1545-0008

b Employer's identification number 0101011	1 Wages, tips, other compensation $14,000	2 Federal income tax withheld $1,626
c Employer's name, address, and ZIP code J & J Personnel Inc. 123 Incorporator Rd. Seattle, WA 99999	3 Social security wages $14,000	4 Social security tax withheld $846
	5 Medicare wages and tips -	6 Medicare tax withheld -
	7 Social security tips -	8 Allocated tips -
d Employee's social security number 000-00-0000	9 Advance EIC payment	10 Dependent care benefits -
e Employee's name (first, middle initial, last) Ella E. Employee	11 Nonqualified plans -	12 Benefits included in box 1 -
910 Work St. Seattle, WA 99999	13 See Instrs. for box 13	14 Other
f Employee's address and ZIP code	15 Statutory employee [X] Deceased [ ] Pension plan [ ] Legal rep. [ ] Hshld. emp. [ ] Subtotal [ ] Deferred compensation [ ]	

16 State	Employer's state I.D. No.	17 State wages, tips, etc.	18 State income tax	19 Locality name	20 Local wages, tips, etc.	21 Local income tax
WA	21212121	-	-			

Cat. No. 10134D

Department of the Treasury—Internal Revenue Service

Form **W-2** Wage and Tax Statement **1995**

For Paperwork Reduction Act Notice, see separate instructions.

security taxes to be withheld and other deductions that may be withheld from employee's wages and the amount of contributions to be made by the employer.

4. Filing federal returns and deposits

Each quarter the Internal Revenue Service mails IRS Form 941 to every corporation. This is the form used for reporting income and social security taxes withheld and the employer's contribution to the social security fund.

Generally, the employer must deposit the income tax withheld plus the employer's and employee's social security taxes in an authorized commercial bank or a federal reserve bank. In addition to filing the IRS Form 941, the federal tax deposit coupon must accompany each Form 941. The computation and requirements for deposits that must be made are printed on the reverse side of IRS Form 941. The amount of taxes to be deposited determines the frequency of deposit.

5. Federal corporation income tax

All corporations except subchapter S corporations and nonprofit corporations are required to pay federal corporation income tax. The corporation tax is 15% of the first $50,000 to $75,000; and 34% of the net profit over $75,000. For net profit in excess of $100,000 the tax is increased by the lesser of 5% of the excess or $11,750. A qualified personal service corporation is taxed at a rate of 34% of its taxable income. If a corporation's taxable income is at least $335,000, it also is taxed at a flat rate of 34% of its taxable income.

The Internal Revenue Service has prepared a booklet entitled *Tax Guide for Small Business*. It is published annually. Get one from your post office or by writing to:

Superintendent of Documents
U.S. Government Printing Office
Division of Public Documents
Washington, D.C. 20402

SAMPLE #29
TRANSMITTAL OF INCOME AND TAX STATEMENTS
(Form W-3)

a Control number 33333	For Official Use Only ► OMB No. 1545-0008		
b Kind of Payer ► 941 [X] Military [ ] 943 [ ] CT-1 [ ] Hshld. [ ] Medicare govt. emp. [ ]		1 Wages, tips, other compensation $14,000	2 Federal income tax withheld $1,626
		3 Social security wages $14,000	4 Social security tax withheld $864
c Total number of statements	d Establishment number	5 Medicare wages and tips	6 Medicare tax withheld
e Employer's identification number 0101011		7 Social security tips	8 Allocated tips
f Employer's name J & J Personnel Inc.		9 Advance EIC payments	10 Dependent care benefits
123 Incorporator Rd. Seattle, WA 99999		11 Nonqualified plans	12 Deferred compensation
		13 Adjusted total social security wages and tips	
g Employer's address and ZIP code		14 Adjusted total Medicare wages and tips	
h Other EIN used this year		15 Income tax withheld by third-party payer	
i Employer's state I.D. No. 0202002			

Under penalties of perjury, I declare that I have examined this return and accompanying documents, and, to the best of my knowledge and belief, they are true, correct, and complete.

Signature ► Title ► Date ►

Telephone number (   )

Form **W-3 Transmittal of Wage and Tax Statements 1995** Department of the Treasury Internal Revenue Service

f. MISCELLANEOUS REQUIREMENTS

1. Business licenses

Many businesses and trades must meet qualifications established by the state, county, and city where the business is located. All of these requirements would have to be met by you even if you hire an attorney to process your incorporation for you.

As the purpose of issuing city and county licenses is mainly to raise revenue, practically all businesses are required to obtain a city or county license. To obtain information regarding a city license, telephone either the city clerk or the city licensing department. Information regarding county licenses is available from the county licensing department or the county tax collector, licensing division. The exact names for these agencies may vary throughout the state, however, an inquiry at the city hall or the county administration office will direct you to the proper agency. For a complete listing of all licenses and other permits needed to start a business, please refer to *Starting a Successful Business on the West Coast,* another title in the Self-Counsel Series.

In Seattle, the application for a business license is filed with the Department of Licenses and Consumer Affairs.

2. Building requirements

All three levels of government have some responsibility for regulating commercial building. Any proposed construction must satisfy all the requirements of the three governments.

The city hall or municipal office brings together all the various building codes and inspections, making it possible for approval of planned construction to be obtained at the local level.

The municipality controls the type of building you may construct. Municipal building and zoning regulations control the physical structure and the final use of your building. The municipality also has the power to enforce building regulations.

Before beginning construction or renovation of a structure, you must obtain a building permit from the municipality. To apply, you must first submit preliminary sketches for approval. When the sketches have received approval, submit complete construction drawings. They will be examined to ensure that they meet the federal, state, and municipal building standards. If approval is given, then you will be issued a building permit.

Once construction has been started, various stages of the construction must be inspected before the project can continue.

As each municipality controls certain aspects of construction, the requirements vary from one area to another, so you should contact the building department of the municipal government office for specific requirements.

3. Patents, copyrights, and trademarks

The laws concerning patents, copyrights, trademarks, and industrial designs are very complicated and you may find professional help useful.

Registered patent and trademark attorneys specialize in these fields, and consulting them will ensure you get maximum assistance.

4. Immigration, citizenship, and customs

If you are established in business in a foreign country but wish to live, work, or establish a business in the United States, you must contact the U.S. immigration representative in your country. See *Immigrating to the U.S.A.,* another title in the Self-Counsel Series.

7

HOW TO REGISTER AN OUT-OF-STATE CORPORATION

If you intend to start business operations in the state of Washington as a branch office of a corporation incorporated in another state, you need to register to do business in Washington with the Secretary of State.

Failure to register will prevent you from initiating legal action or any other operation that requires you to produce official proof of your ability to carry on business within the state of Washington. You would, for instance, be unable to obtain a business license.

To register, you must file an Application for Certificate of Authority to do Business in Washington with the Secretary of State (see Sample #30). One application must be signed in ink by the officer of the corporation, and at least one copy should be filed together with a Certificate of Good Standing, which has been issued within the past 60 days by the appropriate records officer in the home state.

Further, you must file a Designation of a Registered Agent, with a signed consent of the Registered Agent (included in the Certificate of Authority), accompanied by a certified check covering the filing and license fee. A foreign corporation pays the same fees as are prescribed for domestic corporations for filing and annual license fees.

If the corporation name does not contain a corporation designation (e.g., "Inc." "Ltd."), or for some reason the name of record is unavailable for use in Washington, an assumed name must be given. If an assumed name is required, you must attach the Resolution of Directors approving the use of the assumed name.

The law also requires that each foreign corporation file an Amended Application for Certification when there are any changes made. Sample #31 shows one for a name change.

Be sure to file an Initial Annual Report (see chapter 8) along with a certified copy of the Articles of Incorporation that you filed in your state and the Application for Certificate of Authority.

If you simply want to have your corporation name registered so no one else will take it, complete an Application for Reservation of Name (see Sample #5). This will give you the protection you may need on your name until you are ready to begin operations yourself. If you need to renew your registration, you can use the same form.

SAMPLE #30
APPLICATION FOR CERTIFICATE OF AUTHORITY TO DO BUSINESS IN WASHINGTON

STATE of WASHINGTON — **SECRETARY of STATE**

APPLICATION FOR CERTIFICATE OF AUTHORITY TO DO BUSINESS IN WASHINGTON
RCW 23B.15.030

UBI #: ____________________

Phone #: 206-456-7890

Pursuant to RCW 23B.15.030 of the Washington Business Corporation Act, the undersigned does hereby submit this Application for Certificate of Authority.

1. The name of the corporation, as recorded in the jurisdiction of incorporation, is: J & J Personnel Inc.

2. If the corporation's legal name is unavailable or does not meet the requirements of RCW 23B.15.060, the name the corporation adopts for use in Washington is: ____________________

(Note: Attach the Resolution of the Board of Directors approving use of the alternate name.)

3. The state or country of incorporation is: Kansas

4. The date of incorporation was: May 1 199-; period of duration is: [x] perpetual [ ] ___ number of years

5. Has the corporation been doing business in Washington? [x] No [ ] Yes, starting date: ________

6. The street address of the principal office **(wherever located)** of the corporation is:

   Number and Street 123 Incorporator Road

   City Wheat State Kansas Zip Code 88888

7. The name of the person appointed as Registered Agent who resides in the state of Washington is: Robert L. Here

7a. The initial registered office of the corporation, which is identical to the business address of the Registered Agent located in Washington, is:

   Number and Street 1038 Business Row

   City Seattle State WA Zip Code 99999

7b. OPTIONAL - The post office box number, **located in the same city as the physical address**, is:

   PO Box ________ City ____________________ State ______ Zip Code ________

010-001 (1/96)

SAMPLE #30 — Continued

8. **CONSENT TO APPOINTMENT AS REGISTERED AGENT**

I, Robert L. Here, hereby consent to serve as Registered Agent in the State of Washington for the above named corporation. I understand that as agent for the corporation, it will be my responsibility to accept Service of Process on behalf of the corporation; to forward license renewals and other mail to the corporation; and to immediately notify the Office of the Secretary of State in the event of my resignation or of any changes in the Registered Office address.

X RL Here — Sept. 15, 199-

(Signature of Registered Agent) — **(Date)**

9. All current officers and directors names and usual business addresses are:

	Name	Address	City	State	Zip
President	James Doe	123 Incorporator St.	Wheat	Kansas	88888
Vice-Pres.					
Secretary					
Treasurer					
Director	James Doe	123 Incorporator St.	Wheat	Kansas	88888
Director					
Director					

(Attach additional pages if necessary)

10. **Attached is a certificate of existence (or document of similar import), issued no more than sixty (60) days before the application, duly authenticated by the Secretary of State or other official having custody of corporate records in the state or country of incorporation. (Articles of Incorporation do not meet this requirement.)**

11. This application will be effective upon filing unless a date and/or time is specified: ________

(Note: Extended effective date may not be set at not more than 90 days beyond the date the document is stamped "Filed" by the Secretary of State.)

12. This document is hereby executed under penalties of perjury, and is, to the best of my knowledge true and correct.

X James Doe — President — Sept. 15, 199-

(Signature of Officer or Chairman) — (Title) — (Date)

010-001 (1/96)

SAMPLE #31
AMENDED APPLICATION FOR CERTIFICATE OF AUTHORITY TO DO BUSINESS IN WASHINGTON

STATE of WASHINGTON — THE SEAL OF THE STATE OF WASHINGTON 1889 — SECRETARY of STATE

AMENDED APPLICATION
FOR CERTIFICATE OF AUTHORITY
RCW 23B.15.040

UBI #: ______________________

Phone #: 206-456-7890

Pursuant to the provisions of RCW 23B.15.040 of the Washington Business Corporation Act, the undersigned does hereby submit an Amended Certificate of Authority.

1. The name of the corporation, on the records of the Office of the Secretary of State of Washington is: J & J Personnel Inc.

2. The name the corporation currently uses in the State of Washington, if different from its real name listed above, is: ______________________

3. The state or foreign country of incorporation is: Kansas

4. The date the corporation was authorized to transact business in the State of Washington was: Jan. 18, 199-

5. Application is being filed for the following reason *(Check all applicable items)*

   ☐ The corporation has changed its corporate name to: ______________________

   ☒ Name the corporation will hereafter use In the State of Washington is changed to: J & J Personnel of Washington Inc.

   (NOTE: If the corporation is required to use a fictitious name in order to transact business in the State of Washington a copy of the resolution of the board of directors, certified by the corporation's secretary, adopting the ficticous name is attached.)

6. **Attached is a copy of the document filed in the state or country of Incorporation showing that jurisdiction's "Filed" stamp.**

7. This document is hereby executed under penalties of perjury, and is, to the best of my knowledge true and correct.

Dated: Oct. 25, 199-.

X James Doe

(Signature of Officer)

010-002 (1/96)

8

ANNUAL GENERAL MEETING AND ANNUAL REPORT

a. ANNUAL GENERAL MEETING

Large public corporations have a general meeting of shareholders at least once a year and meetings of directors at regular intervals throughout the year.

Ordinarily, your bylaws will stipulate where the annual meeting of the shareholders and directors will take place (see Article 2.3 of Sample #15). If the bylaws do not provide where the annual meeting shall take place, then the meeting is presumed to be held at the registered office of the corporation.

When it shall be held should also be stated in the bylaws (see Article 2.1 in Sample #15). If the meeting is not held, there is no penalty.

Often the minutes of the Annual General Meeting are simply drawn up by the corporation's attorney to reflect the standard procedures that are usually followed, and are sent to the shareholder/directors of the corporation for their signatures.

The practice of holding imaginary meetings can cause problems if dissension arises among the shareholders. Then the whole procedure can be attacked. Also, if you are faced with an IRS audit, the IRS agent will usually ask to review your corporate minute book to check the following:

(a) Are you acting like a corporation?

(b) Did you record important events?

Without a doubt it is good practice to have an actual meeting at least once a year to review the overall situation. Regardless of whether the business is a corporation or not, a meeting of the owners should be held. Even a sole proprietor can sit down with his or her accountant, or lawyer, to examine the results of the previous year and make policy decisions for the ensuing year.

If the Articles of Incorporation or bylaws so provide, a shareholder meeting may be conducted by means of a telephone conference call or similar communications process so that all the shareholders may hear each other at the same time. This law aids compliance with shareholder meeting requirements.

Too often a business stagnates and withers away because it lacks direction and purpose. The retail store goes on selling the same merchandise year after year, ignoring the fact that competitors are aggressively selling new products. Owners can get so busy running in their well-worn rut that they have no time to look around and examine where they have been or where they are going.

At the other extreme, it is not enough for a businessperson to feel assured that, because he or she is constantly alert to all the changes, it is not necessary to stop and consider progress. A change-conscious person who takes the time to hold a meeting might find that his or her course has been erratic because a preoccupation with change has caused a loss of forward direction.

There are also situations where silent partners or minority shareholders never say anything because they are never invited to do so, but they might have some fresh ideas to contribute if given the opportunity.

In contrast, there are minority shareholders who are always complaining about the profit or the general running of the business because they are never informed of the facts. An annual meeting would at least provide the time and place to air all of their complaints at one go and, if it is conducted effectively, the comments might generate positive results which improve the business and reduce future complaints.

While it is not necessary to run a meeting with full dress formality at a board room table, it does help if there is reasonable order and at least a list of subjects set up as an agenda, with one of the persons present appointed as the chairperson to keep the discussion to the point.

Anyone can run a meeting; it does not require an expert! However, a little practice from attending other meetings which are run in formal order can improve the process immensely. Samples #32 and #33 show the standard items of business discussed at the annual shareholders' meeting and the subsequent directors' meeting.

I suggest that you be sure that your shareholders' meeting elect members of the Board of Directors. The directors need not be Washington residents unless the bylaws so require. The Board of Directors' meeting should follow the shareholders' meeting and elect officers. (The positions to be filled, such as President and Secretary, are usually set out in the bylaws — see Article 4 of Sample #15.)

The Board of Directors' meeting should also review important events of the past and the immediate future. Other items to review include the following:

(a) Salaries

(b) Bonuses

(c) Accumulation of surplus

(d) Dividends

(e) Bank resolutions

(f) Medical and dental insurance plans and reimbursement plans

(g) Group life insurance

(h) Fiscal year

(i) Deferred compensation

(j) Major purchases, sales, and leases

(k) 1244 stock issuance

If the shareholders or the Board of Directors are in dispute, then the secretary of the corporation should send written notices to all shareholders and directors of the coming meeting more than ten days before the meeting is scheduled to take place.

The records, minutes, and resolutions of the meeting should be placed in your minute book and kept as a permanent record. I suggest that all record books be kept at the principal place of the corporate business.

In order for a meeting of the shareholders and the meeting of the Board of Directors to be legal, a quorum must be present. A quorum is usually the majority of shareholders for the shareholders' meeting and the majority of the directors for the Board of Directors' meeting. This can be changed by the bylaws or in the Articles of Incorporation.

If you choose not to have a formal meeting, the form shown in Sample #34 illustrates how the shareholders and directors of a company can conduct the usual business by consent of resolution. The resolution, once signed by all directors and shareholders, is filed in the minute book.

b. ANNUAL REPORT

Every corporation is required to file a Corporate License Renewal and Annual Report with the Secretary of State. Your license renewal date will be based on the month of original incorporation or qualification (i.e., if your corporation was filed during the month of May, your license renewal date will be at the end of May each year).

At least 30 days before your renewal date, you will receive a preprinted form from the Business License Center of the Secretary of State's Department of Licensing. You need fill out only the annual report information. If you have a foreign corporation, you will also have to calculate the fees payable by completing the schedule on the annual report form.

After completing the form, it must be sent together with your license renewal fees to:

Department Of Licensing
Business License Center
Olympia, WA 98504

SAMPLE #32
MINUTES OF SHAREHOLDERS' ANNUAL MEETING

MINUTES OF ANNUAL MEETING OF SHAREHOLDERS
OF
J & J Personnel Inc.

The annual meeting of the shareholders was held at the registered office of the Corporation on *February 4, 199-*.

All shareholders were present.

The President gave a report on the business of the Corporation for the preceding year, and after discussion, upon motion duly made, seconded and carried, all actions of the directors were approved, ratified, and confirmed.

The President then called for nominations for directors, and upon motion duly made, seconded and carried, the following were elected directors for the ensuing year:

Jack Doe

John Doe

There being no further business, the meeting was adjourned.

Jack Doe
____
Secretary-Treasurer

ATTEST:

John Doe
____
President

SAMPLE #33
MINUTES OF BOARD OF DIRECTORS' MEETING

MINUTES OF MEETING OF THE BOARD OF DIRECTORS
OF
J & J Personnel Inc.

A meeting of the Board of Directors was held immediately following the annual meeting of shareholders at the registered office of the Corporation on *February 4, 199-*.

All directors were present.

The President then called for nominations for officers, and upon motion duly made, seconded and carried, the following were elected officers for the ensuing year:

President: *John Doe*

Secretary-Treasurer: *Jack Doe*

There being no further business, the meeting adjourned.

Jack Doe

____
Secretary-Treasurer

ATTEST:

John Doe

____
President

SAMPLE #34
WAIVER OF ANNUAL MEETING BY CONSENT RESOLUTION

WAIVER OF ANNUAL MEETING BY CONSENT RESOLUTION

J & J Personnel Inc.

The undersigned, being all shareholders and directors of *J & J Personnel Inc.*, waive the annual general meeting required by Article 2.1 of the Bylaws and consent to the following items of business:

1. That the financial statements prepared and approved by the Corporation's accountant have been presented to each member.

2. That the directors of the corporation for the ensuing year be:

John Doe

Jack Doe

3. That the officers for the ensuing year be:

John Doe

Jack Doe

(OR, in the event of resignation)

2. That *John Doe* has tendered his resignation as director effective this date and that *Jane Doe* was elected as President and director effective this date.

3. That the directors of the Corporation for the ensuing year be:

Jack Doe

Jane Doe

4. That the officers for the ensuing year be:

Jack Doe

Jane Doe

5. That all acts, contracts, proceedings, appointments, and payments of money by the directors and officers of the Corporation since the last annual meeting as appear in proceedings and records of the company be, and the same are, hereby approved, ratified, and confirmed.

6. That the directors and officers of the Corporation are instructed to file all necessary reports and documents. (This refers to the annual report, a sample of which follows.)

WE, the shareholders and directors of *J & J Personnel Inc.*, hereby consent to the waiver of this meeting and we consent to the transaction of such business as would have come before it as testified by our signatures hereto this *4th* day of *February, 199-*.

Jack Doe ______________________ John Doe ______________________

Jack Doe *John Doe*

9

THE CORPORATE HIERARCHY — ALL ABOUT DIRECTORS AND OFFICERS

If you were to visualize the hierarchy of a corporation, it would appear as follows:

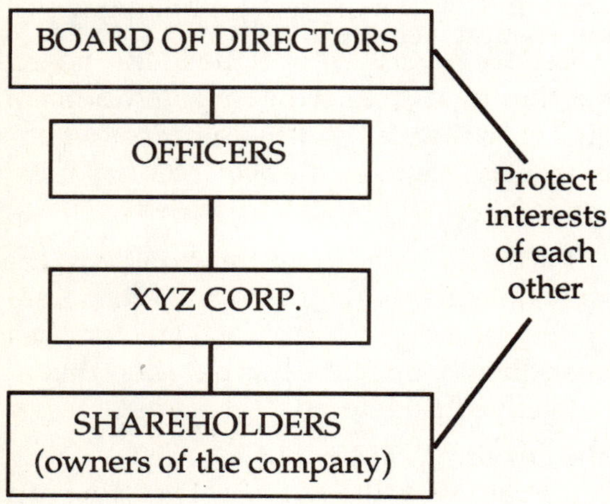

While in theory all corporations look like this little chart, in practice there is a vast difference between how this concept works in public corporations as opposed to small family-owned corporations.

Small corporations can be more accurately described as "close corporations," rather than as corporations as we normally view them, because they usually consist of one, two, or three people who are close personal friends and/or business associates and/or family members. Large publicly owned corporations differ in that the directors, officers, and shareholders are usually separate individuals. The directors on the board of public corporations usually consist of a group of businesspeople, respected in the community, who bring to the board a wide variety of business experience. Their function is to act as "watchdogs" over the officers and to protect the shareholders' interests. Unfortunately, for a variety of reasons, this objective is not always attained. Most officers of a large public corporation are "hired professionals" and they are in charge of the day-to-day activities. In many instances they also wield the greatest influence on the overall operations of the corporation. Usually the two or three top officers of the corporation are also members of the Board of Directors. The largest group in terms of numbers in a public corporation consists of the shareholders, and this group is the theoretical "owner" of the corporation which, in turn, owns the assets. Shares represent "power" in relation to the corporation and its operations.

While in theory final authority for a corporation's operations rests on the shareholders, this can be a myth for various reasons. The shareholders may be widely dispersed geographically, and comparatively few may be able to attend the annual meeting. Also, most people do not buy shares on a stock exchange in the hope of participating in the internal workings of the corporation. They are after two things only — return (dividends) and appreciation in the value of their shares. If they become disillusioned, they do not seek to have management or directors replaced; they simply sell out. In addition, not too many people are competent or knowledgeable enough to have a clear idea of how the day-to-day operations actually work and are not, therefore, in a position to question the activities of management or the Board of Directors. And last, but not least, is the fact that because the shareholders and shareholdings may be widely dispersed, it takes a great deal of time, money, and effort for an individual, or group of individuals, to gain enough support to seriously challenge the members of the Board of Directors and management.

In Washington you need only one director, one officer, and one shareholder, and all of them can be the same person. Be careful not to confuse these positions, even though one person occupies all three. In a close corporation you are often wearing more than one hat at the same time.

To illustrate, in the day-to-day activities of your small business, you are wearing the hat of an officer. If you decide, however, to branch out into a new area, or to purchase or sell assets, you will be wearing the hat of a director. (Important matters which will have considerable effect on the company are always referred to the Board of Directors.) When you attend the annual meeting and vote on the issuing, buying, or selling of shares or substantial assets, you are acting as a shareholder. The shareholder always has the final say on any serious issue because shareholdings represent ownership of the company.

Following are descriptions of the roles, rights, and responsibilities of a director and an officer of the corporation. In chapter 10, the role and rights of the corporate shareholder will be discussed.

a. THE BOARD OF DIRECTORS

The Board of Directors is the traditional governing body of a corporation. In the past, corporate powers had to be exercised by or under the authority of a Board of Directors. The new Washington statute gives you the option of limiting or dispensing with the Board of Directors. RCW 23B.08.010 provides that "a corporation may dispense with or limit the authority of its Board of Directors by describing in its articles of incorporation who will perform some or all of the duties of the board of directors. [1989 c 165 § 80.]"

If the articles or bylaws allow it (our bylaws do not, see Sample #15), the board may have the power to designate, by resolution of a majority of the whole board, a committee of its members to exercise the authority of the board on all but the most significant corporate actions. However, appointing a committee of directors to oversee day-to-day business does not relieve the board of basic responsibility for corporate management.

Unless otherwise specified, the board has the power to elect the corporate officers and to remove any of the officers "whenever in its judgment the best interests of the corporation will be served thereby."

Further discussion in this book will assume that the traditional form of corporate government by a Board of Directors has been chosen.

b. DIRECTORS' MEETINGS

The business of the Board of Directors can be transacted at any meeting of the board as long as a majority (quorum) is present. A meeting may be very informal; the important thing is to draw up the proper minutes and have them signed.

Unless the articles or bylaws provide otherwise, any action required to be taken at a meeting of the directors (or which may be taken at a meeting of the directors) may be taken without holding the meeting if all the directors sign a written consent to the action.

c. DUTIES OF DIRECTORS

Even if your board meetings are held at the kitchen table, your duties are the same as those of directors who sit around a 12-foot teak table surrounded by graphs and plush carpets. A director is required to serve "in good faith," in a manner which the director "believes to be in the best interests of the corporation," and "with such care, including reasonable inquiry, as an ordinarily prudent person in a like position would use under similar circumstances."

1. Good faith

A director is required to act honestly and in good faith and in the best interests of the company. For this reason, a director is prohibited from issuing shares until the company receives full consideration for those shares.

The consideration may be money, past services, or property (land or machinery etc.) The directors may determine the value of the consideration by resolving that in all the circumstances of the case, the property or service is provided to the company at the fair market value. It is no longer possible to issue shares in consideration for someone's promissory note, or future services.

The requirements of acting "in good faith" and in the interests of the company also ensure that directors may not profit personally at the cost of the company. Directors who contract with their company or who have an interest in a contract with the company must disclose to other directors the nature and extent of their interest at the first meeting in which the contract is discussed, or, on failing to disclose promptly to the board, the interested director or officer must disclose his or her interest to the shareholders.

The shareholders must approve the contract by special resolution, and the contract must be fair and reasonable when the company enters into it. This may seem to put a director or officer in a precarious position: the shareholders may approve the contract, but a court at a later date may decide that the contract was not fair and reasonable, so the director may be left wondering for a long time whether or not he or she is entitled to keep the profit from any contract in which he or she was interested.

The duty to disclose is not as onerous as it may seem at first glance because, first of all, it is very easy for a director to disclose his or her interest to friends: the other directors. In this way, no disclosure need be made at all to the shareholders. There is still plenty of room for the principle of "you scratch my back and I'll scratch yours" to operate.

Should disclosure have to be made to the shareholders, very often the largest shareholders are the other directors and, if they approve the contract by special resolution, it will cost some minority shareholders a lot of money to go to court to have the contract set aside on the grounds that it was not fair and reasonable at the time it was made.

Finally, even if the interest of a director or officer in a contract is never disclosed, the contract is still valid until the court sets it aside, or stops its completion on the application of a shareholder or "some interested party." The company itself cannot avoid the contract at its own option.

2. Reasonable prudence

A director must act with the care of an ordinarily prudent person in a similar position. This care includes "reasonable inquiry." In other words, a director must take steps to ensure that he or she is properly informed. A director may rely on information presented by a company officer or employee — which may include lawyers, public accountants, and other professionals — believed to be reliable and competent, or may rely on a board committee upon which the director does not serve as to matters within its designated authority. Regardless, a director is always required to check the information further whenever the need is indicated by the circumstances.

3. Personal liability

What will happen if you either knowingly or unintentionally breach the act and/or your duties as a director? Suppose you declared dividends when your company was insolvent or issued shares to your partner, John Doe, for a promissory note? You have contravened sections of the act and, if the company is proven to have suffered damages as a result of your contravention, you will be personally liable to make up those damages.

If you dissented, and had your dissent recorded in writing, to a resolution approving something which contravened the act, you have a defense and will not be personally liable for any damages. You will also not be held accountable if you can prove that you did not know and could not reasonably have known that the action authorized by the resolution contravened the act. Whether you should have known will be judged on the "man of ordinary prudence" standard.

Suppose you breached the act or your duties and it was either intentional or negligent. All is still not lost. You may obtain shareholder approval for the violation which will absolve you of a breach of your common-law or equitable duties, i.e., to act as a reasonable, prudent person in good faith.

The court may approve and allow the company to indemnify you against any liability you incur, even if it is the company itself that brings the action against you. In order to take advantage of this provision, you must prove that you were acting in good faith, and honestly and reasonably. The court must also feel that you should honestly and reasonably be excused.

The best defense, however, is prevention. Remember that you are bound by the duties of a director even if you are a part-time director or a director who lives outside the state. Take the time to familiarize yourself with the act and the duties under it. Take the time and make an effort to ensure that any board action is authorized under the act and your own articles and bylaws. If you stand to benefit from the action, get director and shareholder approval in advance. The effort spent in preventing trouble will be well spent and you will be rewarded with peace of mind.

d. REMOVAL OF DIRECTORS

Suppose you are the only shareholder and you elect yourself and two friends to the Board of Directors. How can they be removed?

The shareholders can hold a special shareholders' meeting at any time, giving proper notice to all shareholders, and at that time, vote to remove any or all of the directors. No reason need be given. Samples #35 and #36 illustrate what you should use to remove directors.

e. OFFICERS

The officers of the corporation are elected by the Board of Directors. The officers shall consist of a president, one or more vice-presidents, a secretary, and a treasurer. Any two or more offices can be held by the same person, except president and secretary, unless there is only one shareholder in which case she or he may hold all offices. No officer is required to be a director.

Generally the officers' responsibilities are to perform such management duties as provided in the bylaws or as determined by resolution of the Board of Directors. The officers are subject to removal by the Board of Directors.

You should read the previous discussion of directors' duties even if you are only an officer, like a secretary or treasurer, because the same responsibilities are imposed on you.

SAMPLE #35
NOTICE OF SPECIAL MEETING

NOTICE TO SHAREHOLDERS FOR SPECIAL MEETING TO CONSIDER REMOVAL OF DIRECTORS

To the shareholders of J & J Personnel Inc.

The undersigned shareholders of *J & J Personnel Inc.* holding *90%* of all shares entitled to vote, do hereby call a special meeting of shareholders of *J & J Personnel Inc.* to be held at *123 Incorporator Road, Anywhere, Washington,* on the *10th* day of *September, 199-,* at *10:00 a.m.,* for the purpose of considering the removal from office of *Dan Director,* a member of the Board of Directors.

This notice has been mailed by U.S. Post to the last known address of each shareholder of record.

Date: *August 15, 199-.*

By John Doe
100 shares

SAMPLE #36
RESOLUTION REMOVING DIRECTORS

CORPORATE RESOLUTION TO REMOVE DIRECTOR

Meeting of the shareholders was held at *123 Incorporator Road., Anywhere, Washington,* on the *10th* day of *September, 199-,* at *10:00 a.m.* for the purpose of considering the removal from office of *Dan Director,* a member of the Board of Directors.

Upon motion duly made, seconded, and unanimously carried, the following resolution was approved.

RESOLVED: *Dan Director,* is hereby removed from the Board of Directors of said corporation by the affirmative vote of *600* shares.

Jack Doe
Secretary

Approved by:

John Doe
President

10

SHAREHOLDER RIGHTS AND REMEDIES

a. SHAREHOLDERS' MEETINGS

There are relatively few situations outlined in the act or the standard articles and bylaws where a shareholders' meeting is a must. These few situations follow, below.

1. Annual meeting

There must be an annual meeting of the shareholders, although failure to convene one will not necessarily undermine corporate existence. There can be special meetings at any time if proper notification by the Board of Directors, 10% or more of the shareholders, or other person(s) designated in the Articles or bylaws, is given.

Except as limited in the Articles of Incorporation, each outstanding share of voting stock, regardless of class, is entitled to one vote on each matter submitted to a vote at the meeting, and may be voted in person or by proxy. At each annual meeting, the shareholders elect directors to hold office until the next annual meeting, and until their successors are elected and qualified.

Unless otherwise provided in the Articles of Incorporation, cumulative voting for directors shall be a right of each voting shareholder. This means shareholders have the right to multiply their number of votes by the number of directors to be elected at that meeting, and to distribute the total as each sees fit among the candidates.

2. Major corporate actions

Unless the Articles give the Board of Directors the power to adopt, alter, or repeal bylaws for regulation of corporate affairs, this power is vested in the shareholders. Also, the power to amend the Articles of Incorporation is absolutely vested in the shareholders, and changes must be approved by holders of two-thirds of all voting shares.

Other major corporate actions that may not be taken by the directors without more than a majority approval of the shareholders include —

(a) loans by the corporation to its officers and directors,

(b) mergers or consolidations,

(c) sale, lease, exchange, or other disposition of all or substantially all corporate assets, other than in the usual course of business, and

(d) voluntary dissolution of the corporation.

All of these actions require two-thirds approval of the voting shares.

A reduction of the stated capital of the corporation may be approved by a simple majority.

It is important to note that *shareholder approval means approval at a properly called meeting*. One Washington case held that a contract to sell all corporate assets, negotiated by a holder of 88% of the voting stock without a meeting of all shareholders, was unenforceable against the corporation. However, all actions required to be taken by the voting shareholders may be taken without a meeting if all shareholders consent in writing to not holding the meeting and to the action in question.

This is particularly useful in the affairs of closely held corporations.

3. Deep water

You would be wise to call a shareholders' meeting whenever you feel directors are getting into "deep water" because of the extent of your personal liability for your actions as director. A shareholders' mandate would almost certainly validate or excuse any act of the directors on behalf of the company as long as it was done honestly and in good faith.

b. RIGHTS AND REMEDIES

The act gives shareholders broad rights and specific remedies. They can be broken down into the following categories.

1. Access to corporate records

Account books, minute books, and lists of shareholders must be kept by the corporation. Any person who has been a shareholder for at least six months or holds 5% of outstanding shares may inspect these records "at all reasonable times and for all reasonable purposes."

2. Preemptive rights

The phrase "preemptive rights" refers to the right to retain proportionate ownership in the corporation. This right enables a shareholder to purchase a pro rata portion of the most newly authorized stock issued by the corporation, prevent dilution of his or her percentage of ownership, and ensure a continued ability to elect a certain proportion of the Board of Directors.

Shareholders automatically have such preemptive rights unless they are limited or denied altogether by the Articles of Incorporation.

3. Dissent proceedings

Any shareholder has the right to dissent from: a merger or consolidation plan; a sale or exchange of all or substantially all the property and assets of the corporation not made in the usual and regular course of its business, including a dissolution sale (but excepting a sale pursuant to court order); or a plan of exchange where the corporation's shares are to be acquired.

If the action to which the shareholder dissents is approved by the required vote, the dissenting shareholder has a right to have the corporation buy his or her shares at fair market value. The parties must agree on fair market value; if there is no agreement, they can apply to the court for a determination of the question.

4. Representative actions on behalf of the company

A derivative, or representative action, may be brought to protect rights of the minority shareholders, i.e., those controlling less than 50% of the voting shares.

Minority shareholders' suits are an attempt to force the directors (usually the majority shareholders) to do something for the benefit of, or stop doing something that is harmful to, the company and the minority shareholders.

Since it is the company that is supposed to be suffering, in normal circumstances it would be the company that would take the action. However, the minority, not being in control of the Board of Directors, cannot often get the company to act. Consequently, they can sue only as representatives of the company, and the result is that the money recovered in a successful suit belongs to the company and not to the individual minority shareholder who took the action.

You should note the typical practice of awarding the costs of the action to the minority, even if they win. This is rather inconsistent with the idea that the minority is acting on behalf of the company.

Past cases indicate that a minority is entitled to sue in a representative way in the following situations:

(a) When the company is doing or intends to do something which constitutes a fraud on the minority, and the persons controlling the company's activities are the beneficiaries of the fraud

(b) When a resolution has been or is proposed to be passed which requires more than 50% of the voting shares but is or has been passed by only 50% of the voting shares

(c) In any other case where the interests of justice require that the rule be disregarded

5. Involuntary liquidation

The superior courts have power to liquidate the assets and business of a corporation in a shareholder action if it is shown that there is a deadlock that cannot be broken by the directors or the shareholders and the corporation is suffering or is under threat of suffering irreparable damage; the acts of the directors or those in control of the corporation are illegal, oppressive, or fraudulent; or the corporate assets are being misapplied or wasted.

c. TECHNIQUES FOR DIVIDING CORPORATE CONTROL

As indicated in the previous section, the minority shareholder who holds less than 50% of the issued shares is usually in a precarious position in relation to the majority shareholder.

If you are involved in a two-person corporation where the parties are not related (i.e., it is not a family company), the parties should divide the shares equally. If this cannot be done, competent legal advice should be obtained by at least the minority shareholder. If there are substantial assets involved, both parties should seek professional advice.

When there is a basic disagreement over some issue and a deadlock results, either the assets will be sold and the business wound up or one party will buy the other out. This is certainly preferable to the case where the shares are not held equally and the minority shareholder is forced to protect his or her rights by the remedies available under the act.

In other situations, various techniques may be used to reflect the desires of the organizers and major shareholders in the division of corporate power.

1. Share structure and voting rights

(a) Common and preferred stock

One method of varying the statutory pattern of corporate control is through the use of different classes of stock and by varying the rights within the class. An example is to divide the stock into preferred and common stock. When using preferred stock, the rights, preferences, and privileges must be set forth in the Articles of Incorporation.

Normally, the holder of preferred stock would have specified rights over the holder of common stock. For example, a holder of preferred stock may have preferential voting or dividend rights.

(b) Exceptions to preemptive rights

The desirability of preserving the pro rata ownership of the original investors must be balanced against problems arising when additional capital is sought through the sale of stock. Some exceptions to the preemptive right should be kept in mind when considering the adoption of limitations. For example, these rights have been held not to extend to —

(a) stock issued for the sole purpose of purchasing property reasonably required in operation of the corporation,

(b) stock issued in connection with a merger or consolidation with another corporation,

(c) stock issued in connection with payment of a corporate debt, and

(d) issuance of shares.

2. Contracts affecting control

(a) Voting trusts

Any number of shareholders of a corporation may create a voting trust, conferring on a trustee or trustees the right to vote their shares for a period not exceeding ten years. A copy of the agreement must be filed with the corporation at its registered office. Those signing the voting trust agreement are required to transfer their shares to the named trustee. The transferred certificates are canceled and new certificates are issued to the trustee.

The voting trust agreement may be extended for an additional ten-year period. This device is very powerful and has been upheld even, for example, where the practical effect was to deprive a surviving spouse of voting control of community property stock for a period after death.

(b) Shareholder agreements

A shareholder agreement is the usual method for rearranging the statutory scheme for the management of corporate affairs to meet the desires of the participants. Drafting this agreement may be of equal importance to drafting the Articles of Incorporation and bylaws in forming a closely held corporation. Matters often covered by a shareholder agreement include —

- (a) corporate management and variations in voting rights,
- (b) persons to serve as officers and directors,
- (c) employment arrangements and salaries,
- (d) distribution of earnings and timing of possible dividends,
- (e) restriction on stock transfers,
- (f) disposition of stock of deceased or disabled stockholders including valuation technique,
- (g) commitments for future financing,
- (h) commitment of certain participants not to acquire, or to have a right to acquire, an interest in certain competing enterprises,
- (i) arrangements concerning purchase of business insurance by the corporation or the participants or combinations thereof,
- (j) provisions for arbitration or another method of settling potential deadlocks or disputes.

Generally speaking, a Washington business corporation may not prevent shareholders from transferring the corporate stock to whomever they wish. However, the modern tendency is to place restrictions on a free transfer if reasonable and if the shareholder acquired the stock with notice of the restriction. Thus, while an outright restriction against transfer may still cause problems of enforceability, restrictions in small corporations may be upheld if a reasonable transfer procedure is provided. A typical device is to provide for first refusal by the corporation, other shareholders, or both. Adequate notice of the restrictions must be given.

The shareholder agreement also can provide for resolution of a "deadlock." This situation should be defined in the agreement. It may be limited to inability to agree upon matters by a majority of the Board of Directors or inability to make certain defined significant corporate decisions for a specified period of time. Normally the participants will wish to avoid the provisions of RCW 23B.14.300, which gives the superior court power to liquidate the corporation in a deadlock threatening irreparable injury to the corporation.

The typical procedure is to agree upon a third party to serve as an outside director or arbitrator in such a situation.

11
AMENDMENT AND DISSOLUTION

a. CHANGING YOUR ARTICLES

After your corporation is off and running, the need may arise to change (amend) your articles. In most cases this would be a result of changing the share structure to accommodate additional investors.

To amend your articles, an officer of the corporation should complete the Articles of Amendment form (see Sample #37) in duplicate and file it with the Secretary of State's office together with a filing fee of $30. If the amendment increases the capital of the corporation, the fee for the amendment is determined by following the formula shown in Table #1.

The amendment becomes effective upon the issuance of a certificate of amendment by the Secretary of State.

b. DISSOLVING YOUR CORPORATION

Eventually you may decide that it is no longer worthwhile for you to continue doing business as a company because, for example, the directors wish to retire, or substantially all of the assets and inventory of the company have been sold.

1. Washington corporations

A corporation may be involuntarily dissolved; dissolved pursuant to court proceedings; or dissolved by filing the required documents with the Secretary of State. Under the new Washington law, there is a procedure for filing Articles of Dissolution by the initial director(s) or incorporator(s) when no shares have been issued and the corporation has not commenced business (see Sample #38). Otherwise, the corporation may be dissolved by the Board of Directors and shareholders in accordance with RCW 23B.14.020 which requires that the dissolution be approved by two-thirds (or more, if provided in the articles or bylaws) of shareholders entitled to vote. The procedure to be followed with the Secretary of State is the same, that is, the corporation files Articles of Dissolution (see Sample #39). Refer to Table #1 for the fee to submit with your forms.

When you dissolve your corporation, you must keep in mind that there are other requirements (those imposed by the tax authorities, for example) that must be met. Once your resolution for dissolution is passed, all assets of the corporation should be transferred by deed or written documents to their new owners. A dissolved company should own no assets, or future transfer problems could result.

Along with the Articles of Dissolution, the corporation must file an Application for Excise Tax Status for Withdrawal or Dissolution of Corporation (see Sample #40) and a Corporation Guaranty (see Sample #41). Your corporation will not be dissolved by the Secretary of State until you have paid all taxes.

As far as federal taxes are concerned, the IRS requires you to file Form 966 on ordinary dissolution or liquidation within 30 days of the date you adopted the resolution to dissolve. A certified copy of the resolution (one marked with the corporate seal or, if there is no corporate seal, then a copy that the president and secretary sign as being a true copy of the resolution) must be filed along with the form.

Furthermore, all your property payments of social security or employment insurance should be brought up to date and your final submissions marked as final. Many of the forms you use will have a box or line on them where you can make this statement. You will make the same notation on workers' compensation forms filed with the Department of Labor, and on your city or municipal license forms.

I bring these requirements to your attention now so that you will know that a resolution to dissolve your company cannot be taken lightly. A considerable amount of paperwork is required to declare your company legally "dead."

2. Out-of-state corporations

Many of the federal and state tax filings that are required of a local corporation are also required of a "foreign" corporation that did business within the state. For example, you would have to file final employment insurance and workers' compensation payments with the appropriate Washington agencies.

An Application for Certificate of Withdrawal (see Sample #42) would be filed with the Secretary of State's office, instead of the Articles of Dissolution and Statement of Intent to Dissolve. As with local corporations, you would make your filing in duplicate.

SAMPLE #37
ARTICLES OF AMENDMENT

SECRETARY of STATE

ARTICLES OF AMENDMENT
WASHINGTON PROFIT CORPORATION
RCW 23B.10.060

UBI #: ____________________

Phone #: (206) 456-7890

Pursuant to RCW 23B.10.060 of the Washington Business Corporation Act, the undersigned corporation does submit these Articles of Amendment.

1. The name of the corporation as recorded with the Secretary of State: J & J Personnel Inc.

2. The text of each amendment(s) as adopted is (are) as follows:

   Article IV The capital stock of this Corporation shall be $50,000 consisting of 50,000 shares divided into 25,000 Class A preferred voting shares with no par value and 25,000 Class B common nonvoting shares with no par value. Capital stock may be issued by the Corporation from time to time for such consideration, including (without limitation) labor, service, money, or property, as may be fixed by resolution of the Board of Directors from time to time.

   No holder of shares of stock of the Corporation shall be entitled as such as a matter of right to subscribe for, purchase, or otherwise acquire any share of stock of this corporation of any class whether now or hereafter authorized, or any securities convertible into shares of stock of this Corporation.

   (Attach separate sheet, if necessary)

3. If an amendment provides for an exchange, reclassification, or cancellation of issued shares, provisions for implementing the amendment, if not contained in the text of the amendment itself, are as follows:

   ____

   ____

4. The date of adoption of **each** amendment(s) was/were:

   ____

   ____

5. The amendment(s) was (were) adopted by: (Check one of the following statements)

   - [x] The incorporators. Shareholder action was not required.
   - [ ] The board of directors. Shareholder action was not required.
   - [ ] Duly approved shareholder action in accordance with the provisions of RCW 23B.10.030 and RCW 23B.10.040.

6. The document is hereby executed under penalties of perjury, and is, to the best of my knowledge true and correct.

X John Doe	John Doe President	Nov. 15, 199-
(Signature of Authorized Person)	(Type or Print Name and Title)	(Date)

005-002 (1/96)

TABLE #1
FEE SCHEDULE EFFECTIVE OCTOBER, 1994

Office of the Secretary of State
Corporations Division
505 E. Union, 2nd Floor
PO Box 40234
Olympia WA 98504-0234
Information (360) 753-7115

FEE SCHEDULE EFFECTIVE OCTOBER, 1994

EXPEDITED COUNTER SERVICE FEES (in addition to regulatory fees)
For transactions processed at the counter only, on an as staff available basis.

CORPORATIONS, TRADEMARKS, LIMITED PARTNERSHIPS AND LIMITED LIABILITY COMPANIES
Per Entity Name (single or multiple transactions) .... $ 20.00

MISCELLANEOUS FEES

PHOTOCOPIES
CORPORATIONS, TRADEMARKS, LIMITED PARTNERSHIPS AND LIMITED LIABILITY COMPANIES
Any single document (excluding Annual Reports) .... $ 10.00
Articles plus other Charter Documents (excluding Annual Reports) .... $ 20.00
All documents on file (excluding Annual Reports) .... $ 30.00
Each Annual Report .... $ 5.00
(Surcharge for files exceeding 100 pages is $13.00 for each 50 page increment)
TRADEMARK DOCUMENT(S) .... $ .50 per page

CERTIFIED COPIES (fees indicated per each individual document in file)
CORPORATIONS, TRADEMARKS, LIMITED PARTNERSHIPS, AND LIMITED LIABILITY COMPANIES $10.00
plus copying fees above

CERTIFICATES
CORPORATIONS, TRADEMARKS, LIMITED PARTNERSHIPS AND LIMITED LIABILITY COMPANIES
(existence, authorization, record) .... $ 20.00
(long form showing historical data) .... $ 30.00

SERVICE OF PROCESS
SUMMONS AND COMPLAINT (per individual, marital community or entity served) .... $ 50.00

FILING FEES

TRADEMARKS

Registration (6 years) .... $ 50.00
Renewal (6 years) .... $ 50.00
Assignment .... $ 10.00
(New certificate, if requested) .... $ 5.00
Reservation of Trademark (valid for 180 days) .... $ 30.00

LIMITED PARTNERSHIPS

DOMESTIC (WASHINGTON) ENTITIES
Certificate of Limited Partnership $175.00
Certificate of Amendment/Restatement .... $ 30.00
Certificate of Dissolution/Cancellation .... no fee
Reservation of Name (valid for 180 days) .... $ 30.00
Articles of Merger (per entity name) .... $ 20.00

FOREIGN (OUT-OF-STATE) ENTITIES
Application for Registration $175.00
Amendment to Registration .... $ 30.00
Cancellation or Withdrawal .... no fee
Reservation of Name (valid for 180 days) .... $ 30.00
Resignation of Registered Agent .... $ 20.00
Any other Statement or Report .... $ 10.00

ssf 100 (R 9/94)

TABLE #1 — Continued

LIMITED LIABILITY COMPANIES

DOMESTIC (WASHINGTON) ENTITIES	
Certificate of Formation	$175.00
Certificate of Amendment or Restatement	$ 30.00
Articles of Merger (per each listed entity name)	$ 20.00
Articles of Correction	$ 30.00
Certificate of Cancellation or Dissolution	no fee
Initial or Amended Annual Report	$ 10.00
Yearly License Renewal/Annual Report	$ 50.00
Reservation of Name	$ 30.00
Transfer of Reservation of Name	$ 30.00
Any other Statement or Report	$ 10.00

FOREIGN (OUT-OF-STATE) ENTITIES	
Application for Registration	$175.00
Amendment to Registration	$ 30.00
Articles of Merger (per each listed entity)	$ 20.00
Certificate of Cancellation	no fee
Initial or Amended Annual Report	$ 10.00
Yearly License Renewal/Annual Report	$ 50.00
Reservation of Name (valid for 180 days)	$ 30.00
Transfer of Reservation of Name	$ 30.00
Registration of Name	$ 30.00
Any other Statement or Report	$ 10.00

PROFIT CORPORATIONS

DOMESTIC (WASHINGTON) ENTITIES	
Articles of Incorporation	$175.00
Articles of Amendment/Restatement	$ 30.00
Articles of Merger or Exchange (per each listed entity name)	$ 20.00
Articles of Correction	$ 30.00
Articles of Dissolution	no fee
Revocation of Dissolution	$ 30.00
Reinstatement	$100.00
+ back license fees/penalties	
Reservation of Name (valid for 180 days)	$ 30.00
Transfer of Reservation of Name	$ 30.00
Annual License Renewal/Annual Report (including Department of Licensing Application Fee)	$ 59.00
Initial or Amended Annual Report	$ 10.00
Appointment or Change of Registered Agent and/or Registered Office Address	$ 10.00
Resignation of Registered Agent	$ 20.00
Resignation of Officer and/or Director	$ 10.00
Any other Statement or Report	$ 10.00

FOREIGN (OUT-OF-STATE) ENTITIES	
Certificate of Authority	$175.00
Amended Certificate of Authority	$30.00
Articles of Merger or Exchange (per each listed entity name)	$ 20.00
Articles of Correction	$ 30.00
Certificate of Withdrawal	no fee
Reservation of Name (valid for 180 days)	$ 30.00
Transfer of Reservation of Name	$ 30.00
Registration of Name (yearly filing)	$ 30.00
Yearly license Renewal/Annual Report (including Department of Licensing Application Fee)	$ 59.00
Initial or Amended Annual Report	$ 10.00
Appointment or Change of Registered Agent and/or Registered Office Address	$ 10.00
Resignation of Registered Agent	$ 20.00
Resignation of Officer and/or Director	$ 10.00
Any other Statement or Report	$ 10.00

* Reinstatement is not allowed under state law, corporation must requalify

NONPROFIT CORPORATIONS

DOMESTIC (WASHINGTON) ENTITIES	
Articles of Incorporation	$ 30.00
Articles of Amendment and/or Restatement	$ 20.00
Articles of Merger or Consolidation (per each listed entity name)	$ 20.00
Statement of Election	$ 30.00
Articles of Dissolution	no fee
Reinstatement	$ 30.00
+ annual report(s)/fees and $5.00 penalty fee	
Reservation of Name (valid for 180 days)	$ 20.00
Yearly Annual Report	$ 10.00
Amended Annual Report	$ 10.00
Appointment or Change of Registered Agent and/or Registered Office Address	$ 10.00
Resignation of Registered Agent	$ 20.00
Resignation of Officer and/or Director	$ 10.00
Any other Statement or Report	$ 10.00

FOREIGN (OUT-OF-STATE) ENTITIES	
Certificate of Authority	$ 30.00
Amended Certificate of Authority	$ 20.00
Articles of Merger or Consolidation (per each listed entity name)	$ 20.00
Certificate of Withdrawal	no fee
Reinstatement	$ 30.00
+annual report(s)/fees + $5.00 penalty fee	
Reservation of Name (valid for 180 days)	$ 20.00
Transfer of Reservation of Name	$ 20.00
Registration of Name (yearly filing)	$ 20.00
Yearly Annual Report	$ 10.00
Amended Annual Report	$ 10.00
Appointment or Change of Registered Agent and/or Registered Office Address	$ 10.00
Resignation of Registered Agent	$ 20.00
Resignation of Officer and/or Director	$ 10.00
Any other Statement or Report	$ 10.00

SAMPLE #38
ARTICLES OF DISSOLUTION BY INITIAL DIRECTORS OR INCORPORATORS

STATE of WASHINGTON — SECRETARY of STATE

THE SEAL OF THE STATE OF WASHINGTON 1889

ARTICLES OF DISSOLUTION BY INITIAL DIRECTORS OR INCORPORATORS
RCW 23B.14.010

UBI #: ____________________

Phone #: (206) 456-7890

Pursuant to RCW 23B.14.010 of the Washington Business Corporation Act, the undersigned does hereby submits the following Articles of Dissolution.

1. The name of the corporation is: J & J Personnel Inc.

2. Date of incorporation was: Nov. 15, 19-.

3. Check one of the following statements:

   ☒ None of the corporation's shares have been issued.

   ☐ Corporation has not commenced business.

   ☐ No debt of the corporation remains unpaid.

   ☐ Net assets of the corporation remaining after winding up have been distributed to the shareholders, if shares were issued.

4. Dissolution was authorized by a majority of the: (Check one of the following statements.)

   ☒ Initial directors.

   ☐ Incorporators. (Initial directors were not named in the Articles of Incorporation and have not been elected.)

5. A copy of the revenue clearance certificate issued by the Washington state Department of Revenue pursuant to RCW 82.32.260 is attached hereto.

6. These Articles will be effective upon filing, unless an extended date and/or time appears here: ________, 19____.

   Note: Extended effective date may not be set at more than ninety (90) days beyond the date the document is stamped "Filed" by the Secretary of State.)

7. This document is hereby executed under penalties of perjury, and is, to the best of my knowledge true and correct.

   Dated: Dec. 20 19 9-.

X John Doe — John Doe President

(Signature of Person Authorized to Sign) — **(Type or Print Name and Title)**

005-003 (1/96)

SAMPLE #39
ARTICLES OF DISSOLUTION BY BOARD OF DIRECTORS AND SHAREHOLDERS

STATE of WASHINGTON — **SECRETARY of STATE**

ARTICLES OF DISSOLUTION BY
BOARD OF DIRECTOR(S) AND SHAREHOLDERS(S)
RCW 23B.14.030

UBI #: ______________________

Phone #: (206) 456-7890

Pursuant to RCW 23B.14.030 of the Washington Business Corporation Act, the undersigned corporation hereby submits these Articles of Dissolution for the purpose of dissolving the corporation.

1. The name of the corporation is J & J Personnel Inc.

2. The date the dissolution was authorized: Dec. 20, 199-

3. If shareholder approval was required, a statement that dissolution was duly approved by the shareholders pursuant to RCW 23B.14.020 is required.

4. **A copy of the revenue clearance certificate Issued by the Washington State Department of Revenue pursuant to RCW 82.32.260 is required.**

5. This application will be effective upon filing, unless an extended date and/or time appears here: ____________
   (Note: Extended effective date may be set at not more than ninety (90) days beyond the date the document is stamped "Filed" by the Secretary of State.)

6. This document is hereby executed under penalties of perjury, and is, to the best of my knowledge true and correct.

Dated: Dec. 20 199-.

John Doe

(Signature of Person Authorized to Sign)

John Doe President

(Type or Print Name and Title)

005-004 (1/96)

SAMPLE #40
APPLICATION FOR EXCISE TAX STATUS FOR WITHDRAWAL OR DISSOLUTION OF CORPORATION

State of Washington
Department of Revenue AX - 02
Audit Procedures & Administration
Olympia, Washington 98504-0090

APPLICATION FOR EXCISE TAX STATUS FOR WITHDRAWAL OR DISSOLUTION OF CORPORATION

1. Name of corporation: J & J Personnel Inc.
2. Organized under the laws of the state of: Washington
3. Principal place of business in Washington: 123 Business Row, Anywhere, WA 90000
4. Date corporation commenced business in this state: March 15, 1976
5. Describe nature of business in detail: Operation of personnel agency
6. Department of Revenue Registration Number: 10000000. If unregistered, did corporation at any time make sales in or into State of Washington? [ ] Yes [ ] No.
7. If business is to be carried on by successor, state the successor's name: n/a
8. State disposition of the assets of corporation: Sold -- proceeds to creditors; residue divided between two shareholders
9. To see records contact: Name John Doe Phone 123-4567
   Address 123 Incorporator Road, Anywhere, WA 90000
10. No taxable business activities have been conducted, or will be conducted, in the State of Washington after Dec 31, 19 9-.
11. Have all Washington State taxes been reported to the Department of Revenue and the tax liability fully satisfied? [x] Yes [ ] No If not paid, explain:

Provisions for the payment of any license fee, tax, increase or penalty must be made by executing the attached FORM REV 31 0038, Corporation or Individual Guaranty.

12. Proceedings for the dissolution or withdrawal are being instituted before the [x] Secretary of State or [ ] Superior Court; if latter, indicate County__________.

PLEASE NOTE: The Department of Revenue cannot issue its certificate showing that all taxes have been paid or provided for unless the above questions are answered specifically, and in some cases it will be necessary for the Department to perform an audit of the corporation's records before its certificate may be issued.

For Departmental Use Only
R C
By__________

I certify that the above is true and correct to the best of my knowledge.

Signature John Doe

Position President

Date January 15, 199-

FORM REV 31 0037 (7-86)

SAMPLE #41
INDIVIDUAL GUARANTY

State of Washington
Department of Revenue
AuditProcedures and Administration
Olympia, Washington 98504-0090

INDIVIDUAL GUARANTY

IF GUARANTOR IS A CORPORATION, USE OTHER SIDE ONLY

In the Matter of the Dissolution or Withdrawal of

GUARANTY

J & J Personnel Inc.

Each of the undersigned hereby certifies and declares that he has an interest, financial or otherwise, in the above named corporation and is desirous of obtaining from the Secretary of State a certificate of dissolution or withdrawal thereof.

In consideration of the issuance by the Department of Revenue of the State of Washington of its certificate certifying that every license fee, tax, increase or penalty imposed under Chapter 180, Laws of 1935, as amended, has been paid or provided for by said corporation, each of the undersigned hereby agrees to pay to said Department of Revenue upon its demand any and all such license fee, tax, increase or penalty as may hereafter be determined by said Department of Revenue to be unpaid and payable under said act by said corporation.

DATED This 15 day of January , 19 9-

John Doe

Jack Doe

____

FORM REV 31 0038 (5-86)

SAMPLE #41 — Continued

State of Washington
Department of Revenue
Audit Procedures and Administration
Olympia, Washington 98504-0090

CORPORATION GUARANTY

IF GUARANTOR IS AN INDIVIDUAL, USE OTHER SIDE ONLY

In the Matter of the Dissolution or Withdrawal of

GUARANTY

____

It is hereby certified that the undersigned corporation has an interest, financial or otherwise, in the above named corporation and will be benefited by securing from the Secretary of State a certificate of dissolution or withdrawal thereof.

It is further certified by each of the undersigned officers that they have been duly authorized to execute this guaranty for and on behalf of the undersigned corporation.

In consideration of the issuance by the Department of Revenue of the State of Washington of its certificate certifying that every license fee, tax, increase or penalty imposed under Chapter 180, Laws of 1935, as amended, has been paid or provided for by the above named corporation, the undersigned corporation hereby agrees to pay to said Department of Revenue upon its demand any and all such license fee, tax, increase or penalty as may hereafter be determined by said Department of Revenue to be unpaid and payable under said act by the above named corporation.

DATED This____________ day of______________, 19______

By ______________________________
Title or Office

____
Corporation Name

____
Title or Office

FORM REV 31 0038 (5-86)

SAMPLE #42
APPLICATION FOR CERTIFICATE OF WITHDRAWAL

STATE of WASHINGTON — SECRETARY of STATE

THE SEAL OF THE STATE OF WASHINGTON 1889

APPLICATION FOR
CERTIFICATE OF WITHDRAWAL
RCW 23B.15.200

UBI #: ______________________

Phone #: (206) 456-7890

Pursuant to the provisions of RCW 23B.15.200 the undersigned does hereby submit an application for a Certificate of Withdrawal.

1. Name of the Corporation is: Gardner's Greenhouses of Washington Ltd.

2. State or country of original incorporation: Oregon

3. Statement surrendering the corporations authority to conduct affairs in this state: The corporation is not transacting business in the State of Washington and surrenders its authority to transact business in this state.

4. Corporation hereby revokes the authority of its registered agent in Washington to accept service of process, and consents that service of process in any action, suit or proceeding based upon any cause of action arising in Washington during the time the corporation was authorized to conduct affairs in Washington may thereafter be made on the corporation by service thereof on the Secretary of State of the state of Washington.

5. **Attached is a copy of a revenue clearance certificate issued by the Department of Revenue.**

6. Address in the "home" jurisdiction where service of process can be forwarded is: 123 Greenhouse Rd. Small City, Oregon 54321

7. The undersigned does hereby commit to notify the Secretary of State of any changes in the mailing address

8. This document is hereby executed under penalties of perjury, and is, to the best of my knowledge true and correct.
   Dated: Dec. 20, 199-.

X Harvey Gardner
(Signature of Officer or Chairman of the Board)

010-003 (2/96)

OTHER TITLES IN THE SELF-COUNSEL BUSINESS SERIES

STARTING A SUCCESSFUL BUSINESS ON THE WEST COAST

by Douglas L. Clark

$14.95

Create your own job in California, Oregon, or Washington!

With a swelling population and increased trade among Pacific Rim countries, future opportunities for the West Coast look even brighter.

Packed with practical advice and money-saving tips, this book shows you how to start and operate your own successful business on the West Coast. Here are a few of the topics it covers:

- Deciding how to organize your business
- Coping with federal, state, and local laws
- Finding the best location
- How to save money when setting up your business
- How and where to get financing
- How to get help from the government
- Using tax laws to your advantage
- Buying a business or a franchise
- How to find and keep good employees
- How to set up and maintain proper records

Written specifically for first-time businesspeople in California, Oregon, and Washington, the book offers an abundance of information that will prove of continuing value to the new business operator.

BASIC ACCOUNTING FOR THE SMALL BUSINESS

Simple, foolproof techniques for keeping your books straight and staying out of trouble

by Clive Cornish, C.G.A.

$7.95

Having bookkeeping problems? Do you feel you should know more about bookkeeping, but simply don't have time for a course? Do you wish that the paperwork in your business could be improved, but you don't know where or how to start?

This book is a down-to-earth manual on how to save your accountant's time and your time and money.

Inside you will find illustrations of sample forms and instructions on how to prepare all the records you will need to keep, including:

- Daily cash sheet
- Cash summary
- Statement ledger
- Payables journal
- Synoptic journal
- Payroll book
- Income statement
- Trial balance
- Columnar work sheet

Written in clear, everyday English, not in accounting jargon, this guide will help you and your office staff keep better records.

START AND RUN SERIES

START AND RUN A PROFITABLE BED AND BREAKFAST
by Monica and Richard Taylor

This book shows you the business side of opening your home to visitors. It shows you how to plan everything from renovations to record keeping and how to keep your business running trouble-free through its first few years. $14.95

START AND RUN A PROFITABLE CONSULTING BUSINESS
by Douglas Gray, B.A., LL.B.

This practical guide shows how anyone can turn their knowledge and experience into a profitable consulting business. The discussions on all aspects of consulting will get you over the first hurdle of starting your business and direct you toward a profitable marketing plan. $14.95

START AND RUN A PROFITABLE CRAFT BUSINESS
by William G. Hynes, Ph.D.

Those who want to turn their hobby into a money-making project and those who want to improve their current sales will benefit from the dozens of tips in this book. It gives practical instructions for setting up and operating a craft business, whether it is done from the kitchen table or a production workshop. $12.95

START AND RUN A PROFITABLE FREELANCE WRITING BUSINESS
by Christine Adamec

Writing is a business, and to be successful at it, you have to be an effective self-promoter, an able negotiator, a tireless researcher, *and* a talented writer. This book will help you decide whether a career as a freelance writer is for you, and it guides you through each step to success. $14.95

START AND RUN A PROFITABLE GIFT-BASKET BUSINESS
by Mardi Foster-Walker

This book is for people who want to start a gift-basket company as a home-based business or in a rented studio or office space. It gives practical instructions for setting up and operating a gift-basket business, from researching the market to the legal requirements. $14.95

START AND RUN A PROFITABLE HOME-BASED BUSINESS
by Edna Sheedy

Do you fantasize about getting up in the morning and stepping into your office without ever stepping outside? If this is your favorite daydream, this book will help you turn it into reality. It covers topics from running your business without disrupting your family to marketing your product. $12.95

START AND RUN A PROFITABLE HOME CLEANING BUSINESS
by Susan Bewsey

Home cleaning is one of the fastest-growing service businesses in North America. A home cleaning service might start out small, but it has the potential to grow to be a multi-million dollar business. With the help of this book, you can get your business up and running, and survive that essential first year. $12.95

START AND RUN A PROFITABLE OFFICE SERVICE BUSINESS FROM YOUR HOME
by Louise Hagan

If you have experience and training in office services, you can use your skills to be self-employed in your home. The recent explosion of electronic technology has made this possible. $12.95

PREPARING A SUCCESSFUL BUSINESS PLAN

A practical guide for small business

by Rodger Touchie

$14.95

At some time, every business needs a formal business plan. Whether considering a new business venture or rethinking an existing one, an effective plan is essential to success.

Using worksheets and a sample plan, readers learn how to create an effective plan, establish planning and maintenance methods, and update their strategy in response to actual business conditions.

Contents include:

- The basic elements of business planning
- The company and its product
- The marketing plan
- The financial plan
- The team
- Concluding remarks and appendixes
- The executive summary
- Presenting an impressive document
- Common misconceptions in business planning
- Your business plan as a tangible asset

From start to finish, this working guide outlines how to prepare a plan that will win potential investors and help achieve business goals.

STANDARD LEGAL FORMS AND AGREEMENTS

Steve Sanderson, editor

$14.95

This book provides a wide selection of indispensable legal forms and common business agreements ready to be copied and filled in with the particulars of the arrangement.

- New businesses — agreement of purchase, partnership agreement
- Services — engagement of services
- Employment — employment agreement, employee dismissal letter
- Buying — invitation to quote, cancellation of purchase order
- Selling — bill of sale, limited warranty
- Collections — request for payment, bad check letter
- Credit/Debit — personal credit application, guarantee
- Leases — commercial lease, agreement to cancel lease
- Assignments — assignment with warranties

All samples are provided full-size in this large format volume with lay-flat binding, so no fussing with enlargements is necessary and copying is both easy and perfect quality.